LEADERSHIP DEVELOPMENT PROGRAM

Guide to Christian Faith

Readings in Youth Ministry

Edited by John Roberto

THE WORLD OF
DON BOSCO
MULTIMEDIA

New Rochelle, NY

Other books in the
Leadership Development Program:

Guide to Youth Ministry Programming

Guide to Understanding Youth

Foundations of Leadership for Youth Ministry:
Leader's Guide

Prepared in Conjunction with
The Center for Youth Ministry Development

Guide to Christian Faith
©1991 Salesian Society, Inc. / Don Bosco Multimedia
475 North Ave., P. O. Box T, New Rochelle, NY 10802
All rights reserved

Library of Congress Cataloging-in-Publication Data
Guide to Christian Faith/ edited by John Roberto.
p. cm. — (Leadership Development Program)
Includes bibliographical references.
    1. Christian Faith   2. Youth—Religious life.
      I. Roberto, John.   II. Title: Guide to Christian Faith.   III. Series.

ISBN 0-89944-160-2 $ 4.95

Printed in the United States of America

10/91   9 8 7 6 5 4 3 2 1

CONTENTS

PREFACE

The *Leadership Development Program* meets a critical need in youth ministry — the development and training of volunteer leaders for ministry with youth. A vibrant youth ministry relies on well-equipped volunteer leaders to build relationships with youth, to share faith with young people, and to organize and conduct programming. The *Leadership Development Program* is designed to assist diocesan/regional leaders and pastoral leaders, like the coordinator of youth ministry or director of religious education, to train volunteer leaders for their ministry.

A *Foundations of Leadership for Youth Ministry* manual provides the trainer with 25 complete training designs, background materials, and worksheets to teach each of the 25 topics covered in the three *Guide* books. The three *Guide* books provide essential reading and practical ideas that volunteer leaders need to be effective in their ministry.

The *Leadership Development Program* can be used in a variety of different ways. The *Foundations* manual with the training designs and *Guide* books can be organized into three, eight or nine session weekly programs, or into three weekend training programs, or into multiple full-day training programs. They can also be used one at a time according to the needs of the volunteer leaders. The *Guide* books have been designed to accompany the training sessions *and* as stand-alone books for individual reading and use by the volunteer leaders.

Guide to Understanding Youth is designed to help leaders better understand adolescent growth and development and learn ways to promote growth and development. Topics in this *Guide* include: early adolescent growth, older adolescent growth, adolescent faith development, families with youth, social context of adolescence, youth culture, ministry with racial/ethnic minority youth, and contemporary ministry with youth.

Guide to Youth Ministry Programming is designed to help leaders understand the theory *and* to develop practical skills for designing effective youth programming. Topics in this *Guide* include essays on how to design: community building activities, storytelling and faith sharing activities, evangelization activities, learning experiences, worship experiences, prayer activities, justice programs, and service/action programming.

Guide to Christian Faith is designed to help leaders better understand the basics of the Christian faith and how this faith is shared through relationships and programming. Topics in this *Guide* include: Old Testament, Gospels, Jesus and discipleship, Church and ministry, sacraments, moral decision-making, Catholic social teaching, and Catholic identity.

ABOUT THE AUTHORS

Lawrence Boadt, CSP is associate professor of Sacred Scripture at the Washington Theological Union, author of *Reading the Old Testament* and other books, and has a doctorate in Biblical Studies and Near Eastern Languages from the Pontifical Biblical Institute.

Sandra DeGidio, OSM is president of the Servants of Mary religious community, the author of *Enriching Faith through Family Celebrations* and *Sharing Faith in the Family*, and a lecturer in the field of family catechesis/ministry, liturgy and Christian initiation.

Leonard Foley, OFM has served as associate editor of *St. Anthony Messenger* and editor of *Weekday Homily Helps*, and as teacher, parish priest, and retreat master. He is also the author of several books, including *Believing in Jesus*.

Thomas Hart, PhD teaches theology at Seattle University and is a marriage and family counselor in Seattle. He is the author of *To Know and Follow Jesus* and *The Art of Christian Listening*.

Norman Langenbrunner, a priest of the Archdiocese of Cincinnati, is a high school religion teacher, a part-time religious studies instructor at the University of Dayton, and a parish priest.

Nicholas Lohkamp, OFM holds a Doctorate in Sacred Theology and is the author of several articles and books, including *Living the Good News*. He has taught theology at the college and graduate level and gives retreats and workshops on morality across the country.

Richard McBrien teaches in the department of theology at the University of Notre Dame, a priest of the Archdiocese of Hartford, Connecticut and author of fourteen books, including the *Catholicism*.

Joseph Martos heads the theology department at Allentown College in Pennsylvania, is the co-author of *Why Be Catholic?* and the author of several books on the sacraments, included *Doors to the Sacred*.

Richard Rohr, OFM, founder of New Jerusalem Community in Cincinnati, now serves as executive director of the Center for Action and Contemplation in Albuquerque, New Mexico. A popular lecturer and author, whose most recent work is *Why Be Catholic?*

ACKNOWLEDGEMENTS

"Approaching the Bible" first appeared as "How to Understand the Bible" by Norman Langenbrunner in *Catholic Update* (UPD 032), 1982. This is reprinted with permission of St. Anthony Messenger Press.

"Approaching the Old Testament" first appeared as "Themes of Old Testament Theology" in *Reading the Old Testament* (1984) by Lawrence Boadt and is reprinted courtesy of Paulist Press.

"Approaching the Gospels" first appeared as "How the Gospels Were Written by Leonard Foley, O.F.M. in *Catholic Update* (UPD 053), 1983. This is reprinted with permission of St. Anthony Messenger Press.

"Jesus and Discipleship" first appeared as "Christian Discipleship" in *To Know and Follow Jesus* (1984) by Thomas Hart and is reprinted courtesy of Paulist Press.

"Church and Ministry" is excerpted from "What is Ministry" in *Ministry: A Theological, Pastoral Handbook* by Richard McBrien and is reprinted courtesy of Harper and Row.

Excerpts from *Called and Gifted* by the Catholic Bishops of the United States are taken from *Called and Gifted: The American Catholic Laity* (November 13, 1980) and is reprinted courtesy of the United States Catholic Conference, Office of Publishing.

"Sacraments" first appeared as "The Seven Sacraments — Symbols of God's Care" by Sandra DeGidio, O.S.M. in *Catholic Update* (UPD 043), 1983. This is reprinted with permission of St. Anthony Messenger Press.

"Moral Decision-Making" first appeared as "Your Conscience and Church Teaching" by Nicholas Lohkamp, O.F.M. in *Catholic Update* (UPD 1282), 1982. This is reprinted with permission of St. Anthony Messenger Press.

"Moral Decision-Making and Personal Discernment: A Catholic Approach" is excerpted from *Human Sexuality: A Catholic Perspective for Education and Lifelong Learning* by the Catholic Bishops of the United States (November 21, 1990) and is reprinted courtesy of the United States Catholic Conference, Office of Publishing.

"Catholic Social Teaching" is excerpted from *A Century of Social Teaching*, a Pastoral Message of the Catholic Bishops of the United States (November 29, 1990) and is reprinted courtesy of the United States Catholic Conference, Office of Publishing.

"Catholic Identity" first appeared as "Eight Good Reasons for Being Catholic" by Joseph Martos and Richard Rohr, O.F.M. in *Catholic Update* (CU 0888), 1988. This is reprinted with permission of St. Anthony Messenger Press.

Typist: Alicia Carey
Artist: Jeanne Bright

INTRODUCTION

All of our programs, activities, and relationships with youth are designed to promote their continuing growth in Christian faith — deepening their relationship with Jesus Christ. The greatest gift that you can offer young people is your Christian faith and values — your faith journey, your relationship with Jesus Christ, your continuing efforts to live faithfully as a disciple of Jesus Christ. You become a role model for what being a Christian means today. This challenge means that we must continue our growth in faith — in both our understanding and practice of the Christian faith. Your continuing growth is at the heart of an effective ministry with youth.

The *Guide to Christian Faith* is designed to help you better understand the basics of the Christian faith, to feel more comfortable with contemporary understandings of the Christian faith, and to discover how to share this faith through your relationships and in your programs. This *Guide* will provide you with tools for interpreting the Bible, with an overview of the key themes of Old Testament, with an understanding of how the Gospels developed, with an overview of the life of Jesus and the requirements of discipleship, with a summary of the Church's mission and contemporary approach to ministry, with a contemporary look at the sacraments, with an overview of Christian moral decision-making, with the key themes of Catholic social teaching, and with the major emphases of Catholic identity today.

The Guide to Christian Faith is designed as an overview for adult leaders. Each of these chapters can serve as enrichment for you *and* as the basis for evaluating current programming or designing new programming with youth.

1
APPROACHING
THE BIBLE

WHERE I STAND

1. The Bible is important in my life as a Christian because...

2. The Bible was composed primarily to...

3. Interpreting the Bible is difficult because...

4. In order to understand the meaning of a passage or book of the Bible I...

5. The Church assists me in interpreting the Bible by...

READING   NORMAN LANGENBRUNNER

The problem of interpreting the Bible remains a great stumbling block for many. Catholics are conscious that the Church has some very definite ideas about certain teachings and stories in the Bible. The fear of misunderstanding a passage and being led astray by private, unguided interpretation is very real. St. Jerome, still considered the Church's greatest biblical scholar, issued this stern warning over 1500 years ago: "Farming, building, carpentry, etc., all require an apprenticeship, but when it comes to interpreting God's Word...any doddering old fool or dilettante can blithely dissect it and have a go at explaining it — masters in their ignorance!"

Many Bible readers are intimidated by the technical language of Scripture scholars and confused about the methods currently used in interpreting the sacred texts. Terms such as "literary form" and "exegesis" are unfamiliar to many who studied the Bible in the past. This essay is designed for those who want a clearer understanding of what Scripture scholars are teaching today. Used alongside the Scriptures, this summary supplies basic information which the Bible reader needs to pursue the Word of God with confidence, understanding the spiritual benefit.

HOW MOST SCHOLARS APPROACH THE SCRIPTURES TODAY

The modern approach to studying the Bible can be traced back to the 17th century when a French Catholic priest named Richard Simon published a three-volume work entitled *A Critical History of the Old Testament*. Applying the techniques of literary and historical analysis to the sacred texts, Simon concluded that Moses was not the sole author of Genesis. He found that unwritten traditions actually preceded the written texts by several centuries. Although attempts were made to suppress his work even before it was published, Simon's study of the Old Testament marked the start of a more critical, more scientific approach to the Scriptures.

Because it makes use of historical research, literary analysis, and the findings of archaeology, anthropology and other sciences, this modern approach to the Bible has been called the Historical-Critical Method. It is historical inasmuch as scholars seek to discover the social, economic, political and cultural setting of biblical times. It is critical in that experts judge and evaluate the text and its narrative in the light of literary analysis and scientific information. Through this kind of scholarly detective work modern Bible readers are interpreting what the ancient Bible writers had to say.

Most serious scholars today believe that the Bible is God's Word in human terms. They do not reject inspiration, but neither do they believe that God dictated the words of Sacred Scripture to secretaries or mere human tape recorders. Rather, God's people experienced God's holy presence, learned the divine will, and then found the means appropriate to them to express, under God's inspiration, the truths of this revelation. Through the Historical-Critical Method we have come to see that the Bible in no way contradicts the truths of reason or the facts of science.

The Historical-Critical Method employs several types of criticism, investigating the literary form, the origin of a text or story, the historical details and so on. Listed below are the chief types of criticism or analysis which modern scholars use.

MODERN TOOLS OF INTERPRETATION

Textual Criticism. Scholars begin their work with the handicap of not having the original text of any book of the Bible. All we have are copies, made years after the originals. The task of the textual critic is to verify as much as possible that the copies we have are accurate reproductions of the missing originals. Through painstaking comparison of ancient manuscripts, the textual critic corrects errors which have crept into the copies and establishes which manuscripts contain the most primitive forms of the sacred text.

Form Criticism. The form critic tries to identify the literary form which the biblical author has used. Like our newspapers, the Bible contains various kinds (genres) of writing. Each literary form of genre (narrative, fiction, drama and so on) has its own rules for composition and presentation of the truth. Poetry, for example, allows greater freedom of expression than does history. If the reader fails to recognize that the literary form of a text is poetry, he or she may well come away with a faulty interpretation. Imagine the confusion of anyone who reads the description of the bride in the Song of Songs, but fails to consider the literary form: "Your hair is like a flock of goats...your teeth are like a flock of ewes...your neck is like David's tower..." (4:2-4).

Genesis 1:1—2:4 provides us with a different kind of literature. By analyzing the Creation story in the light of literary forms of archaeological discoveries, bible scholars have come to realize that this first chapter of Genesis is based upon an ancient *myth*. Unfortunately most modern readers consider "myth" to be equivalent to "fairy tale" — a good story perhaps, but without truth. This understanding of myth, however, is totally different from what the sacred writer and biblical scholar intend.

A myth is a human way of exploring and dealing with a mystery. The people of Israel did not know *how* the world was made, but they were convinced that it was their God *who* made it. Without the advantage of telescopes and satellites, the sacred writer had to settle for a less scientific way of expressing his faith conviction that Jahweh was the Creator. Borrowing an old Babylonian myth, *Enuma Elish*, the Jewish author stripped the story of its specifically pagan elements and used what was left to express his belief. Under the form of sacred myth, he tells a beautiful story of Creation, dramatically expressing the truth of God's power, goodness, wisdom and love. Today's science and technology show us a different picture of the physical origins of our world. But the truth of the biblical account is as firm as ever: Jahweh made the heavens and the earth and all they contain.

Source Criticism. It is the task of the source critic to discover the origin of the materials which the biblical authors used to tell their story. The history in the books of Kings and Chronicles is probably based upon the court records dutifully preserved by the royal scribes. The Psalms are songs and prayers gathered by the priests and people for official Temple worship. In the Pentateuch (the first five books of the Bible), scholars believe that there are at least four major traditions, drawn from stories handed on by word of mouth.

For example, evidence in the first chapter of Genesis indicates a *Priestly* source, developing during and after the time of the exile (584 B.C.) and preserving the traditions associated with worship and the Temple. It is this "P" tradition which emphasizes the Sabbath day, for "God blessed the seventh day and made it holy..." (Gn 2:3).

And older source, known as the *Jahwist* tradition because it prefers to call God by the name "Jahweh," is responsible for most of the second chapter of Genesis. Readers who compare the story of Creation in Chapter 1 with the story in Chapter 2 can detect a change in the order of Creation, the addition of God's name in 2:5 ("Lord" or "Jahweh"), and differences in language and style. Because of its focus in Jerusalem, this "J" tradition is probably from the southern part of the kingdom, about 10th century B.C.

A third source can be seen in Genesis 20. Here and in other passages of the Pentateuch, we find a vocabulary and style which indicate a northern tradition. Scholars have dubbed this source the *Elohist* or "E" tradition and believe it developed around Samaria after the Schism in 922 B.C.

The fourth source is the *Deuteronomist*, named for the tradition and style found in the book of Deuteronomy. Although the Priestly tradition presents a code of law in Leviticus, a second, more homiletic presentation of the Hebrew law is preserved in the "D" source. By determining the source of the story, the critic can demonstrate the reliability of the narrative and assist in the correct interpretation of the passage.

Redaction Criticism. This brand of criticism focuses on the editing of the biblical books. "To redact" means "to edit or adapt for publication." Some unknown editor or editors gathered the sources, selected materials and wove them into the biblical accounts. Sometimes the editor put similar stories back to back, as he did in the two stories of Creation (Gn 1:1—2:4a and 2:4b-25). Other times he wove two accounts of the same story together, as he did in the story of Noah and the flood. Genesis 6:11-13 is repetitious of Genesis 6:5-8, both sections telling of God's displeasure with human wickedness.

In the New Testament we find two stories of Jesus' birth, the one of Matthew (1:18—2:12), the other by Luke (2:1-19). The redaction critic asks why the two evangelists using the same basic material have told significantly different stories. Here, as in most cases, it is the editor's purpose and audience which give use the clue to his choice of material and his presentation of it.

Historical Criticism. With the help of archaeology, history and dating techniques, the historical critic determines the age of a document or text and verifies the information found in the biblical record. Historical criticism has shown, for example, that the book of Wisdom, although attributed to King Solomon, was actually written several hundred years after his death. Scholars have shown that the author of Wisdom was familiar with the *Septuagint*, a Greek translation of the Hebrew Scriptures, done in the second century B.C., about 800 years after Solomon died. The language and style of Wisdom suggest, in fact, an author living in the first century B.C., probably a resident of Alexandria in Egypt.

Use of these five branches of the Historical-Critical Method has received the approval of several popes over the last 100 years. From Leo XIII's encyclical *Providentissimus Deus* in 1893, which initiated the new era in Catholic biblical studies, to Pius XII's *Divino Afflante Spiritu* in 1943 and the Vatican II constitution *De Revelatione* in 1965, Catholic scholars have been urged to pursue the study of the Bible with all the modern tools available to them.

INTERPRETING THE SCRIPTURES

With the information supplied by the Historical-Critical Method, biblical scholars are in a better position to pursue the task of correctly interpreting the written Word of God. Such scholarly interpretation of the Bible is a science technically known as *exegesis*. This term simply means "the explaining or interpreting of a text." The exegete applies certain principles to the task of "drawing out the meaning" of the Scriptures.

These principles form the so-called *hermeneutical process*. ("Hermeneutics" is a term derived from the name of the Greek messenger god Hermes and generally refers to the principles of interpretation and human communication.) The exegete first determines the literary form of the passage and then applies the principles of the hermeneutical process in order to determine what the author meant by the words he chose.

Most Catholics and Protestants, for example, are agreed that Mark 3:32 should read "the brothers and sisters" of Jesus. Catholics, believing in the perpetual virginity of Mary, point out that "brothers" can refer to "cousins, relatives or associates." Many Protestants on the other hand do not hold to Mary's perpetual virginity and so understand that Mary must have had other children besides Jesus. Both Catholic and Protestant scholars agree that either interpretation is possible based upon this verse alone. In this case a scholar's interpretation will depend on evidence from outside of the biblical text. Catholics thus point to the ancient tradition that Mary was a virgin even after the birth of Jesus. Nothing in the biblical text contradicts that tradition.

THE ROLE OF THE CHURCH IN INTERPRETATION

Catholics maintain that the Church, especially the College of Bishops, whom they believe are the successors of the apostles, has the authority to authentically interpret divine revelation. Jesus sent his Spirit to lead the Church to truth (Jn 16:13), and that Spirit remains the guide to and guarantor of the truth of God's Word. In practice the Catholic exegete recognizes that the essential beliefs of the Church are a most helpful guide to correctly interpreting a biblical passage. Church teaching serves as a kind of "checks and balance" system for the scholar's interpretation. The Church, as American scholar Father Raymond Brown sees it, is "par excellence the place where Scripture is heard in its truest and fullest meaning."

Very few of the Bible's verses have been solemnly interpreted by the Church's hierarchy, but popes, bishops, theologians and preachers turn to the Scriptures with great frequency to demonstrate and highlight the truths of faith. Those who seek to "prove" religious beliefs or settle arguments by appealing to the biblical texts are seldom successful in convincing their adversaries. The freedom of interpretation which some Christian denominations allow and the official interpretations which other Churches promulgate, usually produce a stalemate, a no-win situation when two opposing sides clash.

FUNDAMENTALISM

Not all Bible enthusiasts accept the Historical-Critical Method. Some of the more conservative Protestant denominations reacted to what they considered a too liberal, too rational approach to the Bible. This reaction became known as *fundamentalism*. According to this position, the Bible must be accepted literally, in its obvious sense, and should not be subjected to any kind of scientific and historical analysis. "If God says he created the world in six days," they insist, "then that's the way it happened. Evolution contradicts the Bible and therefore cannot be true."

Many of the radio and TV preachers were hear on Sunday morning are fundamentalists. They refuse to recognize the Bible's use of literary forms. By appealing to passages in the prophets and in the Book of Revelation, they develop elaborate prophecies about future famines, catastrophes, wars and the end of the world. To ignore the historical context in which the biblical books were written is to open the door to all kinds of fanciful and unwarranted interpretations.

The Historical-Critical Method, on the other hand, helps us take a more balanced view of the written Word of God. Without denying the truth or inspiration of the Scriptures, the modern exegete is in a better position to determine what scholars call the *literal sense*, that is, what the biblical author intended to say with the words he used. The failure to recognize hyperbole (exaggeration), sarcasm, myth or other literary forms easily leads to false interpretation and the danger of making the Bible say things it was never intended to say.

A BOOK OF FAITH

The Bible was not composed to teach science or catalog historical facts. It is above all a book of faith. A group of people recognized God's presence in their community, recorded their experiences over several centuries and eventually collected and edited those traditions into the one volume we call the Bible. Through the pages of this book modern believers continue to experience the Lord whose loving presence has been a constant throughout all of salvation history.

Aided by the research of archaeologists, historians, experts in ancient literature and other scientists, Historical-Critical scholars have explained the sacred text and helped modern believers to grasp its message. Popes and councils have urged scholars not to stop at the scientific investigation of the Scriptures, but to go on to the work of promoting and supporting the faith of Christian readers. Thanks to the findings of modern biblical scholarship, 20th-century believers continue to see that all Scripture "is inspired of God and is useful for teaching...and training in holiness" (2 Tim 3:16-17).

HOW I GROW

1. The most important insights I learned about understanding the Bible...

_____
_____
_____
_____
_____
_____
_____
_____
_____
_____
_____

2. Ways I can use these insights in my life and in my ministry...

_____
_____
_____
_____
_____
_____
_____
_____
_____
_____

3. Questions I need to explore in future learning:

_____
_____
_____
_____
_____
_____
_____
_____
_____
_____

2

APPROACHING
THE OLD TESTAMENT

WHERE I STAND

1. The Old Testament is important in my life because...

2. For me, the most important theme communicated in the Old Testament is...

3. The image of God in the Old Testament that I found most appealing is...

4. Understanding the Old Testament is difficult because...

5. The book of the Old Testament that speaks to me the most is...

READING
                                    LAWRENCE BOADT

The Old Testament is such a rich book, written over many centuries by many different authors, and containing such a wide variety of Israel's religious traditions, that readers often have difficulty finding any threads to *unify* it. The same reaction may have struck us as we read about the early books of the Pentateuch and then turned to the prophets or wisdom sections. In order to appreciate the whole Bible, it is very important for us to be able to discover some unifying themes which make this a single Testament of faith *and* which enable us at the same time to treasure its many different voices expressing the breadth and beauty of the human experience of God over the ages.

The first question biblical theologians ask of the Old Testament is whether there is one *viewpoint* that characterizes all the books. Some have said that its central theme is *historical* — that is, the Bible tells the factual story of God's interventions into human history on behalf of the Israelites. This would not be ordinary history, but a special "salvation history" which concentrated attention on moments when God revealed himself in certain *events* or in the giving of divine words for human guidance through Moses or the prophets. Other scholars suggest that the major thrust is that of a "proclamation" or "confession" of God. It is Israel celebrating its relationship with God. This view especially takes account of how much of the Old Testament is not *historical* in nature, but rather *praise* and *questioning* — for example, the Book of Psalms or Job or Ecclesiastes. If it is "confession," then we must ask a further question, "Does the Old Testament have a *single* central theme that is proclaimed?" Some possible ones might be God's *choice* of Israel above other peoples, or the lasting *covenant* that God made with Israel, or God's *holiness* manifest in the world, or the *promise* which runs through both Old and New Testaments.

But those who emphasize the historical nature of Israel's traditions, and those who emphasize its proclamation of God's relationship, emphasize important truths, and to select one exclusively over the other would be to lose much of the power of the Scriptures. Israel was an intensely *historical* people; and more so than any of its neighbors, it was conscious of where it had come from and what had happened to it in different moments of its past. But it made that awareness of history alive by announcing the continual praises of God, and in living an established way of life that challenged every new generation.

The only fair candidate for a single dominant theme in the Old Testament would be the *person of God*. The implied questions — "Who is God?" "What does God do?" "Why does God do it?" — fill every page and every level of tradition of the Bible. Naturally, the Old Testament is also the story of the people Israel, for this one God interacted with them, and they began to understand God through their experience as a people. But it is not primarily the story of God and Israel *alone*. Although the people remembered what God had done for them, they also spoke about what God does for the *whole* world and all its nations. The Bible testifies to the universal greatness and love of God. Israel made no claim that God acted only on its behalf, nor did it insist that its knowledge of God was *entirely* special and revealed only to itself. In several passages of the Bible, Israel acknowledges the insights *other peoples* have had by borrowing their language and thoughts. One example is the flood story of Genesis 6-9, another is the description of God as Lord of the storm like Baal, found in Psalm 29.

Because Israel had a strong sense of God's special intervention into its history, it saw its duty both to *remember* the wonderful things God had done for it alone and to *proclaim* and affirm the truth about this God to the whole world.

THE ONLY GOD

Thus the *first and most important* theological theme found in the Old Testament is that *God is one*. This may seem like a small statement, but it governs everything. Israel lived in a world with many competing gods and many debased ideas about divine power. The polytheism of its neighbors was based on an attempt to understand the forces of nature and the mysteries of life that faced humans every day. Why is there drought, sickness and death? How do we find blessing of good crops, children, security and peace? The common answer was to recognize different divine powers everywhere, often with the competing aims and attitudes toward human beings. The means of relating to these gods was, in effect, to *manipulate* them into doing what we needed or wanted. Elaborate rituals and rites that *imitated* the force of storms or the generating acts of sex gradually led to an attitude toward divine beings as glorified humans complete with all our envies, pettiness, moods and self-interest. The world and its gods were nearly identical. In contrast, Israel insisted on a single divine being who ordered and controlled everything out of love for the goodness of creation. The creation story in Genesis 1 makes this clear. And God never acted from whims nor tolerated immoral behavior as part of worship — Genesis 2 and 3 make this clear. Nor were there to be any rivals nor struggles of other forces threatening to overwhelm God — the flood in Genesis 6 and the tower of Babel story in Genesis 11 make this clear. Above all, this God ruled human history and actively guided, protected, cared for and was involved in human affairs — the whole Bible tells this story. It affirms everywhere that God was never to be confused with the created things of the world. The Old Testament returns again and again to the themes that God is *holy*, God is *King*. God is *Shepherd* or *Father*, God is *Creator* — always to emphasize the transcendence of God. God is near the world but never of it. As Jeremiah 23:23 puts it, "Am I a God nearby, says the Lord, and not a God far away?" "Do I not fill heaven and earth?" Perhaps the highest point in Old Testament theology is reached in the famous prayer of Deuteronomy 6 on this very point: "Hear, O Israel, the Lord our God is one Lord, and you shall love the Lord your God with all your heart and with all your spirit and with all your power."

GOD ACTIVE IN HISTORY

This brings us right to the heart of the *second important theological theme* in the Old Testament. God is an actor in history. Israel is literally created by the action of God. God reveals that history is not neutral, but is a stage for the discovery of the self-revealing God. Israel thus proclaims that pagan ideas of circular time, those unending repeating cycles of events in which nothing is every really new, must be discarded for good. History is *ever new*, it moves ahead, and we can grow better or worse in it, and we can certainly learn from it. This insight flows from the worship and adoration of a transcendent God. If God is not merely part of nature, tied to its ups and downs and its wet seasons and dry, God can act *upon* it. Some years ago, the term "salvation history" for the Old Testament was very popular. It expressed the sense that Israel remembered and learned from those moments when God acted in the events which were most crucial to its past existence. But theologians are now less willing to use that term, because it fails to call attention to the vital element of worship and philosophizing that makes up a large part of what the Bible says of itself. At the same time, we should not totally lose sight of this "salvation history" approach because it underscores Israel's breakthrough insight that God not only *cares about* humans but operates in a carefully *ordered* and loving way for the *good* of humans — and always has.

Above all, this insight into divine activity declares that God was a *Liberator and Savior*. God delivers the patriarchs Abraham, Isaac and Jacob; God saves Moses and the slaves at the Red Sea; God hears the cry of the poor and listens to them in the Psalms; God frees the servant who gives witness through suffering in the Book of Isaiah; God pleads with Israel to return and change its heart and be liberated in Hosea and Jeremiah. There is perhaps no stronger theme anywhere in the biblical tradition than this one. It forms the background for understanding the New Testament proclamation of Jesus; it is the *central motif* of the later themes of *messiah* and *hope*. And it certainly has vital ramifications for our world today.

PERSONAL RESPONSE AND PRAYER

The *third important theological theme*, which follows from the second about God as *actor in time*, asserts the necessity of *human response* to what God does. The Old Testament never accepts that a worship of God can be adequate which is grateful only for the preservation and daily working of nature. Ours is a personal God who demands from us a *personal* response of friendship, loyalty, obedience, and communication. In Scripture this truth takes many forms. It can be seen in the passages that recognize God's "glory" in the world, or in the Temple in Jerusalem, and that lead Israel to awe and wonder. It takes shapes in the spirit of trust and even complaints freely offered that form the fabric of the Psalms. It makes possible the existence of the great prophets who not only speak in God's name but watch over and *insist upon* concrete replies by Israel in both deeds and words. The very creation of the Bible as a sacred book stems from the awareness that Israel must express itself fully before God — both in the telling of its story and in the constant praise of the living and present God in its midst, and even in the rather both and daring questioning by wisdom writers who seek to understand their relationship with God more deeply.

Our *fourth theme* is really a concrete application of this human response — *prayer* — or the *praise of God*. The Bible is history and cate-chetics, speculative thought and poetry and entertaining tales and much more, but all of it is praise of God. Israel was a community that learned to place its purpose and hopes and self-understanding only in God. So when we read the Scriptures, we should not consider just the Psalms as our prayer. *All of the biblical texts* tells the glory of God. It is not always easy to see praise of a good God in the violence of Joshua or Judges, or in the doubts of Job and Ecclesiastes; but Israel saw God present in blessing even there, and could still pray in the midst of a very real sense of curse all around them. Today many people would like to blot out the harshness of human sin and divorce God from it, and demand of God an end to injustice before they give praise. Instead, the Bible teaches us something about our continual need to struggle for what is right while proclaiming that only God can accomplish it.

COVENANT AND TRADITION

The *fifth theological theme* might be called *community and covenant*. The Old Testament came into existence as the remembering by an on-going community who received what had been the testimony of others and took responsibility for it. Above all, they clung stubbornly to a conviction that God had indeed entered into a special relationship of *covenant* with them — a covenant that established bonds of loyalty and responsibility between God and humanity in the person of Israel. It is our task to recognize how this formed and preserved the true *inner bond* of Israel as a *community* which maintained a profound respect for the worth and love of the neigh-bor — as Leviticus 19:18 points out so strongly when it demands *love of neighbor* as much as of oneself.

A *sixth important theme* follows from the last one. Israel is above all a people of *tradition and institutions*. It is *Torah*, "teaching" or, even better, "way of life." Israel does not shrink from including laws regarding sacri-fice and regulations about bodily ailments and sanitary practices right next to moral and ethnical demands for justice and humility and caring. The Old Testament is a rather awkward collection of materials because it reflects *all* the different sides of life in community. We should keep in mind that the traditions come from a very long period of time, at least a thousand years, and probably much more. Anyone who has seen the musical "Fiddler on the Roof" knows the importance of tradition to keeping alive a sense of community in a difficult and often hostile world.

The greatness of biblical revelation is that it uses the structure of society to help a community function religiously, but at the same time moves beyond these structures. Thus Israel could demand *fidelity* and *obedience* to God's law that no other Near Eastern monarch had to face. Or it could demand from individual tribes a cooperation and submission of their own purposes for the good of all Israel. When the Assyrians destroyed the northern kingdom of ten tribes, the rest could progress to a new understanding that God worked even when you did not have the Promised Land to inhabit; and when the Temple and king were destroyed by the Babylonians, they perceived that these too were dispensable, and that God would now act in new ways. The Scriptures themselves are written so that Israel can be freed from any single human social structure or government or land and continue to meditate and proclaim the *enduring covenant* through time.

THE PROPHETS AND JUSTICE

A seventh significant theme that follows from an honest wrestling with Israel's sense of concrete existence in the world is found in the *tension between God's will and our often sinful and selfish response*. Israel was no pollyanna that thought of human nature as always good and God as always forgiving of any and every fault. The Israelites never failed to proclaim God to be a God of mercy, as Exodus 34 expresses it, "slow to anger and rich in kindness," but they tempered it with a true awareness of *justice*. God does indeed make demands on the community, demands that they be *like* God. If the claim of Genesis 1:26 means anything when it says that humans are made in the image and likeness of God, it means that we too have moral choice and moral responsibility. Leviticus 19 insists over and over that Israel obey God's laws because God is *holy*. If God indeed faithfully treats the world in an ethical and right fashion, acting solely out of love and goodness, then the *proper* human response must be in kind.

This explains the central vitality of *prophecy* to the Old Testament tradition. The prophets are the *ethnical watchdogs* par excellence. They should not be seen only as radical innovators or rebels against the laws and traditions. They recalled tradition to the people, showing them how God had acted in the past, and what the covenant had taught, and insisting that Israel not forget the freedom of God to act in new ways or the faithfulness of God that would not overlook repeated violations of the covenant. The prophetic word indeed stands in judgment on Israel's behavior only because Israel *forgets*. Ethics is therefore not divorced from the great sense of tradition but stands within it. There is no picture of God in the Hebrew Scriptures, unlike in many of the pagan myths and prayers, that ever *forgets* that he is a God of *action* who demands *actions* in return. God always acted rightly, and all Israel must act rightly because they remember as their sacred duty what God is. "Forgetting" negates the meaning of history and establishes evil practices because they seem helpful or useful for our present desires. Prophecy challenges these. As a result, prophecy has often been seen as a highlight of Old Testament revelation, and perhaps it is, but, if so, only because it roots itself forcefully in the covenant and narratives of the Pentateuchal revelation.

HOPE AND THE FUTURE

That the office of the prophet was watchdog and critic and challenger of Israel's evil ways is balanced by the fact that the prophetic office also brings comfort and hope in times of trouble and loss. This itself is the *eighth theological theme: hope and optimism* about the future. Biblical theologians often speak about "eschatology" in the Bible and mean by it the dynamic expectation that God will act in the future. This is not just the natural assumption that God will work tomorrow as God did today, but the much greater confidence that God has all of time and human history under a plan and that there will be moments of profound change when God intervenes. This conviction took shape in any number of crisis moments facing Israel in the Old Testament — the rise of the kings in the tenth century, the loss of northern Israel and ten of 12 tribes in the eighth century, and the loss of land, Temple, king and independence in the sixth century. Never in any of these crises did Israel come to the conclusion that God would *not act* again. They interpreted disasters as punishment for their own evil for the most part, and the prophets frequently warned the people that God had future punishment in mind if they would not *convert* their ways. But there always remained a conviction, even when the prophets used the most absolute and damning language condemning Israel, that God would *renew* or *restore* because above all God was faithful.

This led to the hope of a *messiah*, a figure sent by God, greater than any king of the past, who would bring about the full flowering of Israel. Such hopes were really quite late in the Old Testament period and are only mildly reflected in the actual books of the Bible — an example is Daniel — but were very common among other writings and in Jewish groups just before the time of Christ. As Christians think of the Old Testament's relation to the New, they must be careful not simply to say that Jesus *fulfilled* all the unfulfilled messianic words of the Hebrew Scriptures. Jesus acted differently than even the Old Testament expected and revealed what the Israelites always knew through the prophets — God *does not do* what you hope for; he acts in new and surprising ways. We cannot expect it, but we must know God well enough to *accept it.*

The sense of hope should be coupled with *another theme — the goodness of the world* and of the creation that God has made. Hope is rooted ultimately in the knowledge of a good God. Israel has many beautiful passages in its Scriptures that express this deep conviction of God's majestic power and blessing on all of creation. It can be found in the creation story of Genesis 1 and 2 in the blessing that God brings on the earth, and the fact that for each day of the creation story, God "saw that it was good." it can be seen in the blessing and promise themes to Noah, Abraham, Isaac and Jacob, in the wisdom poems of Job 28 or Proverbs 8 or Sirach 24, and in the overwhelming imagery of praise in the Book of Psalms.

Many scholars wondered why the Bible had so little to say of an *afterlife.* Only in one of the latest books of the Bible, Daniel, does such a belief emerge clearly. Perhaps Israel focused itself so strongly on the covenant with the *now-community* that it had little room for wondering how that bond could be continued after death. But eventually the radical belief that *God was good* without fail — from beginning to ultimate end — led to an equal assertion that God could raise the dead who had suffered unjustly — could preserve the faithful Israelite into the life to come. It remains a minor theme in the Hebrew Scriptures but takes a much more central place in light of the resurrection of Jesus.

THE MYSTERY OF GOD'S WAYS

Finally, we should conclude with a *last theme of importance:* the Bible is *wisdom.* Wisdom books are not just appendages but form a very important layer of tradition that affirms that God made humans *rational and free*, with divine powers of *searching* and *choosing* and behaving ethically. Wisdom writings boost the goodness of being human and seek to explore dimensions of God and the problem of relating to God that troubled everyone. Israel never developed philosophers like the Greeks who exalted human reason as a power that answers to nothing but itself. Israel maintained that the *search* for wisdom *must be done* in awe and fear of the Lord. Greeks were skeptical of how the gods could actually interact with the created world. Israel *never doubted* how active and directly present God was to the world. Israel's wisdom thinkers instead turned the believers' questions and difficult problems of suffering and inequalities among people toward the *mystery of existence.* God's ways were not our ways, and while we can see God at work we cannot understand with our insights the what or why. But covenant love for the one God demanded both proper reverence for divine transcendence and bountiful hope for divine nearness.

The legacy of the biblical traditions of Israel that have been brought together in the Scriptures is a *combination* of divine *nearness* and *distant* greatness, of intimate, individual love side by side with reasonable, orderly governance. These ten theological themes help bring this out about the God of Israel. Continued reading and study of the Old Testament will serve to nourish these truths more deeply and to open up innumerable *other aspects* of our relationship to God.

HOW I GROW

1. The most important insights I learned about understanding the Old Testament...

_____
_____
_____
_____
_____

2. Ways I can use these insights in my life and in my ministry...

_____
_____
_____
_____

3. Questions I need to explore in future learning:

_____
_____
_____
_____
_____
_____
_____

3

APPROACHING
THE GOSPELS

WHERE I STAND

1. The Gospels are important in my life because...

2. For me, the most important teaching communicated by the Gospels is...

3. The image of Jesus in the Gospels that I find most appealing is...

4. Several reasons for the different approaches of the four Gospels are...

5. The most difficult Gospel teaching for me to live is...

READING   LEONARD FOLEY, OFM

In this essay, I will try to summarize some of what responsible scholars have said about the formation of the Gospels. Where do we start our exploration of how the Gospels were written?

Since this is written for Christians, we must start with the central event of Christian history and Christian faith: *the resurrection of Jesus*. If ever the expression, "It blew their minds," is proper, it is apt to describe what happened to the followers of Jesus as they experienced the risen Jesus and then began to realize who that mysterious, attractive man really was — *is*.

Suppose you struck up a conversation about the Normandy invasion of World War II with an old gentleman on a park bench — and later learned you had been listening to General Omar Bradley? Or, to put it over-bluntly: What would you and your friends do if you found out later that the *man* on whom you had staked your lives was — *God*? To say the least, once you experienced Jesus as the risen Lord, you would see his every word and action in a profoundly new light. You would start reminding each other about what he had said about this and about that.

At the same time, other followers of Jesus would also gather to remember and retell. The sick would remember some days more fondly, sinners others. Those who would have to debate publicly would remember what suited their need. If you were hungry, you would remember bread. If you were being ground into poverty, you would remember the Beatitudes, the story of the rich man and Lazarus.

The Church in Jerusalem might emphasize the cleansing of the Temple and not recall Jesus' going to the Gentiles. In Galilee, the Church might stress the stories that centered around the lake and merely summarize Jesus' baptism down in Judea.

The point is, memory would be sharpened by need, by personal experiences, by local conditions. Some things would be emphasized in one place and not even recalled in another.

The stories of Jesus would be told at the gatherings for Eucharist. Gradually there would be collections of stories, told and retold over the years. Scholars have found that folk memory preserves detached units best; for instance, general sayings of Jesus apart from any particular situation; or stories that lead up to a punch line (e.g., "Give to Caesar what is Caesar's, but give to God what is God's" — Mk 12:13-17); or narratives with almost no words of Jesus, but colorful details centering on a miracle (e.g., the storm on the lake — Mk 4:35-41). The units were told in patterns that made them easy to remember. As time went on, these separate units would be polished to smoothness like stones in the daily tide.

When the first Christian preachers went forth, it was not with tape recorders and movie projectors. They proclaimed *the meaning of Jesus* in terms the people could understand, in the Jewish way to Jews, in the Greek way to Greeks.

The only "bible" they had was what we call the Old Testament, the Hebrew Scriptures. *They found Jesus in its pages.* He was the fulfillment of all that had been promised. His life, death and resurrection were "according to the Scriptures." But they were gradually (many without realizing it) building up what we call the New Testament, at first in oral and then in written collections. By saying the final result was *inspired*, we mean that the Holy Spirit guarantees the truthfulness and trustworthiness of what human beings said and wrote *in human ways*.

THREE LEVELS IN THE BIBLE

For Catholics, the problems of the human side of the Bible were immeasurably clarified by a landmark statement of the Pontifical Biblical Commission in 1964 which recognized the advances in biblical scholarship.

In summary, the document states that Bible interpreters "should pay diligent attention to the *three stages of tradition* by which the doctrine and life of Jesus have come down to us"; in other words, to the way the Gospels were formed and finally written down. These three stages are: 1) what *Jesus himself* said and did; 2) what the *apostles* preached; 3) what the various *"sacred authors"* were each trying to accomplish. Each of these elements, not just the first, had an important bearing on what turned out to be the New Testament as we know it today.

First stage: Jesus' own words and actions. He "followed the ways of reasoning and explaining in vogue at the time," says the Biblical Commission. He was a man of his time. He used the manner of teaching — and of debating — followed by the rabbis. He had his own purpose, for instance, in telling the parable of the sower. He preached the same Good News in many places, not always in the same words. He emphasized one thing to the poor, another to the hypocritical religious establishment, another to the sick. He wrote nothing down.

In the last sentence of his Gospel, St. John says, "There are still many other things that Jesus did, yet if they were written about in detail, I doubt there would be room enough in the entire world to hold the books to record them" (Jn 21:25).

Second stage: The apostles' preaching. *The apostles* proclaimed the death and resurrection of Jesus and explained his life and words, "taking into account in their method of preaching the circumstances in which their listeners found themselves." In other words, the apostles *adapted* and *interpreted* Jesus so that their hearers would understand as fully as possible who he was and what his life and death and resurrection *meant* for their eternal salvation.

And, the Biblical Commission adds, they preached *"with the fuller understanding which they enjoyed."* They did not merely repeat the words of Jesus; they proclaimed the meaning of the words and actions of the God-man in the light of their fuller knowledge and experience. The Holy Spirit did not print words on their imaginations' blackboard, but showed them the ever-deepening *meaning* of Jesus. The words they used to preach and teach were their own.

The apostles had "their own purpose"; they spoke in a way that "suited the mentality of their listeners." They used different *forms* of expression. (All Bible scholars recognize varying "literary forms" which each require different interpretation — exactly as every day people recognize the difference between [and different interpretation of] valentines, movie scripts, contracts, New Year's resolutions and editorials.) So the apostles used "catechesis, stories, hymns, doxologies, prayers — and other literary forms accustomed to be used by men of that time."

Jesus' words and actions received a new light, a new depth and a fuller interpretation than was possible before the Resurrection and the coming of the Spirit. They were passed on in new situations, and according to the mentality, culture and need of new hearers. In other words, the apostles inevitably *interpreted* Jesus.

Third stage: The authors' actual accounts. We see now a twofold source for the Gospel writers: namely, the original stories — sometimes taken word for word into the Gospels from oral tradition — and also the fuller interpretation of Jesus as it appeared in the preaching of the apostles. The third stage now takes place in the attempt of writers to "compile a narrative," as Luke says in his introduction, "of the events which have been fulfilled in our midst."

All four Gospels have the same general purpose, of course. But each Gospel has its own style and flavor because four different authors and traditions were at work. Mark, for instance, concentrates on what Jesus did rather than on what he said, and on his suffering humanness rather than his divinity. Matthew is the Christian rabbi intent on catechesis. Luke has an eye for Jesus' mercy, for Christian prayer and renunciation, and for the poor. John presents a majestic, divine Jesus, and a Kingdom of salvation already in force.

WHY THE DIFFERENT APPROACHES?

We can discern several reasons for the rich difference of approach in the four Gospels:

First, each writer *selected* some stories and sayings rather than others, according to his individual purpose and viewpoint. The "seven last words" of Jesus are not all together in any one Gospel: Luke has three of them, Matthew and Mark share one, John has the other three. Matthew has eight beatitudes; Luke has only four, but he parallels them with four woes. John has no account of the institution of the Eucharist. The baptism of Jesus is progressively deemphasized in the four Gospels. The Our Father is slightly different in Luke and Matthew. All this is the result of the authors' varying emphases and intentions.

Second, the Gospel writers, speaking for and in the Church, and following the practice of the Church, shaped the words of Jesus, *adapted* them to apply to new situations, ones that did not exist when Jesus spoke. We have seen that the apostles themselves did this. Jesus would not have said, to *Jews*, for instance, that a woman could not divorce her husband (Mk 10:12). This was unheard of in Jewish law. But among Greeks it was possible, so Jesus' full meaning had to be expressed.

Matthew and Mark describe Jesus as dying with a loud cry, but they do not record any words. In Luke, Jesus said, "Father, into your hands I commend my spirit" (23:46). Some scholars feel that Luke's expression of trust is parallel to "My God, my God, why have you forsaken me?" in Matthew (27:46). In John, Jesus said, "Now it is finished" (19:30). They are three artists painting the same sunset.

The Gospel writers often had to vary their accounts because the communities for which they wrote were so different.

Some were widely scattered, some in totally pagan areas, some close to the Jerusalem tradition, some being persecuted, some living in peace. For converts, certain questions had to be asked. For Greeks, certain Jewish customs had to be explained.

Other examples of new situations:

* Jesus is called "Lord" by persons who did not *then* know or believe he was God. Even the apostles took a long time to realize who Jesus was. It took the Church a long time to decide how to *define* the Trinity: three "persons" in the one "nature" of God.

* In John's Gospel we no longer find the harassed, beaten and suffering Jesus. Now we meet a Jesus who speaks as though he is already in glory. It is not he who is on trial; it is the world. He is master of the situation, serene, powerful. There is no agony in Gethsemane in John. Rather, a cohort of soldiers falls down merely at his word.

* Even the *place* where a Gospel writer puts a story may depend on his purpose. John has the cleansing of the Temple at the beginning of Jesus' public life; Matthew at the end. The Biblical Commission notes this fact: "Since the meaning of a statement also depends on the *sequence*, the Evangelists, in passing on the words and deeds of the Savior, explain these now in one context, now in another, depending on their usefulness to the readers."

In short — and this is obviously a statement with far-reaching implications — the Biblical Commission says that the Gospel writers "express Jesus' sayings *not literally but differently*, preserving their meaning."

To sum up, then: While there is a vast amount of similarity in the Gospels (especially the first three), the individual writers did not have their own purposes, and employed techniques of selection, adaptation, modification. It should be evident that the Gospels are not mere *"lives of Jesus."* They are the Church's attempt to proclaim to various people in various situations the *meaning* of Jesus. The Gospels should not be seen as photographed-tape-recorded biographies.

THE GOSPELS: A RECORD OF FAITH

What shall we call them, then? Perhaps it would be best to use the phrase "faith-record" with the following analogy in mind. Suppose you have four brothers and sisters, and after your mother's death, they ask you (a writer) to "put Mother on paper." They want you to tell the way she really was, in words that express all she meant to the family and to others and also to convey her spirit. So you sit down and decide what great qualities of your mother you want to highlight. She was, among other things, a very hospitable person. You never knew how many people would be there for dinner. So you present a few typical scenes. You describe one evening meal where there was present the pastor, six boy scouts and a knight of the road who happened to be passing by. Now, actually it was the assistant pastor, four members of John's swim team, and the knight of the road was there the same time as the bridge club. It wasn't Coke she gave the kids, but Nehi — a pop they don't even make anymore. Why explain? But the cheerful openness of your mother comes through.

You remember your mother as cracking a joke just before she died. One of your brothers, a very proper person, reminds you that it wasn't a joke, just a mildly humorous remark—but he grudgingly admits that if she had thought of the joke she would have told it. So when you're finished your brother and sisters say, "That's our Mom! You have *her* just the way she really was!" (Even though you said that party was in summer when actually it was winter. But you needed to describe how she took all the guests outside later and served ice cream—as she did on 20 other occasions.)

So we do not approach the Gospels the way the IRS would approach your tax report. Rather, *the Gospels are testimonies of faith addressed to those who are the faithful.* They cannot be used to "prove" anything to pagans or scientists or Hindus.

Remember, it was a *loving* group (no matter how undependable and obtuse of mind) that listened to Jesus. The Gospels are not the Pharisees' notion of Jesus, but the picture that developed in the minds of those who loved him, the community we call Church.

We must remember that *it was the Church who wrote the New Testament* (just as it was the Jewish people who wrote the "Old") — this loving group of followers. They painted the masterpiece gradually, a touch here, a touch there, as an artist gradually puts his subject on canvas. Individual authors (probably a succession) put their stamp on the finished product, but the Word of God was heard and written within the faith of the community. Privately, we may develop some highly distorted versions of reality. But in a group, a real community, we get our corners knocked off — and that can be called inspiration too.

It is, therefore, important to remember that the Gospel writers did not go off to their ivory towers to write. Though they each had their own purposes, they were expressing the basic faith-record that had been developed in the meditation and prayer of the Church and by the light of the Holy Spirit.

The Church rejected whatever accounts did not have an authentic ring to them — there are several noncanonical gospels filled with marvelous accounts of supposed incidents in Jesus' life. But these were not incorporated into the New Testament.

FINDING THE LIVING JESUS TODAY

It is a living Jesus, speaking to each new situation, that the Church of the first century described. The Gospels present the same Jesus today, but garbed, as it were, in the robes of a Jewish rabbi, using the thought-forms of a man of his day. We must find the living Jesus for today in the Gospels, just as the early Church found the Jesus of their day in all the oral tradition that gathered around him.

We do not read the Gospels to amass information — a good novelist could probably do a splendid job for us, if that's all we wanted. But we pick up the Gospels, love letters of the Church, with reverence and anticipation, to be addressed by the living Jesus *now*. This cannot be done in a simplistic way, however. Faith is not enough to understand Jesus' words and actions. We must let wise men and women instruct us.

This is not to say that ordinary people cannot find a clear and simple message — and meet God — in many verses of the New Testament. But a comprehensive and balanced view is important.

Just as we need to know the circumstances of the time to fully understand the American Constitution written in 1787, so we need to know *what the Gospels meant to the people who wrote them down*. Then we can know the meaning of Jesus and his message today.

HOW I GROW

The most important insights I learned about understanding the Gospels...

_____

_____

_____

_____

_____

_____

_____

_____

_____

_____

Ways I can use these insights in my life and in my ministry...

_____

_____

_____

_____

_____

_____

_____

_____

_____

_____

Questions I need to explore in future learning:

_____

_____

_____

_____

_____

_____

_____

_____

_____

_____

4

JESUS
AND DISCIPLESHIP

WHERE I STAND

1. For me, Jesus is...

2. For me, following Jesus means...

3. Some of the outstanding features of Jesus' life and ministry include...

4. In the Gospels Jesus teaches...

5. My relationship with Jesus challenges me to...

READING   THOMAS HART

Jesus does not just save us. He calls us to follow him. He does not just comfort us; he challenges us as well. What Jesus began in his life is not yet finished. He inaugurated the reign of God, but he asks our help in bringing it to completion. The following of Jesus is called discipleship. A disciple is literally a learner or student. The call is to assimilate the teaching of Jesus and imitate his example. It is to labor with him for the transformation of the world.

Discipleship does not stand next to salvation as a separate topic. It stands within it. To live the Gospel is already to be saved in considerable measure. One has found the way, the truth, and the life. One knows the joy of Jesus in following his path, living in union with God in love. One is no longer lost but has been found. No longer enslaved in habits of sinfulness, one has turned away from death to life. True, one is not completely saved.

But Christian discipleship is the way which leads to life, both in this world and in the next. And Christian disciples help bring God's saving love to all humanity.

It is on Jesus that we must concentrate our attention if we wish to grasp the contours of Christian discipleship. He models the way of life, and he teaches it. Let us examine the main features of his life and teaching. Then let us look at some of the ways discipleship can go astray. Finally, let us speak of friendship with Jesus Christ as the heart of discipleship.

JESUS' LIFE

1. **He Lives for God.** The most striking feature of the life of Jesus is how totally centered it is in God. Out of his own "Abba experience," which we will describe more fully later on, Jesus names God "Father," and draws close to him. This is the God Jesus wants to share with us. "Father" is a metaphor. It does not mean that God is masculine. The metaphor could as easily be "Mother." The God of Jesus is gentle, nurturing, faithful, tender, creative, compassionate. The idea of the metaphor, which arises from human experience, is that God is like a loving parent, the best conceivable, and that we can relate to God in love and trust, knowing that we are accepted and cared for. Jesus lives his whole life before this God. He trusts God, even when trust is hardest. He sees God's creative hand and providence everywhere. He speaks of God freely and often. He seeks opportunities to be alone with God in prayer. Jesus' whole objective is to do God's will, to accomplish God's work. Jesus *is* attractive and compelling as a human person, and probably almost everything about him would appeal to an atheist. But Jesus certainly cannot be explained, or even adequately described, without his relationship to God. God is everything to him.

2. **He Lives for Others.** Open the Gospel to almost any page, and you will find Jesus dealing with someone. It might be an individual, it might be a crowd, but in the scene Jesus is doing something for someone. He is forgiving sins, healing diseases, freeing people from their fears, feeding a crowd, calming a storm, teaching or answering questions, inviting or encouraging someone. He might also be confronting religious and political leaders, but even this will be in the interest of oppressed people. The Lutheran theologian Dietrich Bonhoeffer calls Jesus "the man for others." He is devoted to relieving human misery. He spends himself in service. What is amazing in Jesus is the universality of his love, his reverence for all persons no matter who they are, his ability to see the good, his desire that all people enjoy inner and outer freedom and fullness of life.

When we look for cues as to how to live the Christian life, it is important to note that Jesus is a man in the midst. He is not an ascetic or a recluse. He leads no desert movement and counsels no one to "leave the world," though he tells us we are not "of the world" (Jn 17:15-16). We find him in some Gospel frames seeking lonely places to be with God, but always he returns to service, which remains the dominant note. His prayer seems to serve his ministry, even that longest prayer of his, the 40 days in the desert, from which he emerges to begin his public life. In his public life Jesus is chided for not fasting, as John the Baptist and his disciples fast. He earns instead the name of "glutton and drunkard, friend of tax collectors and sinners" (Lk 7:34) for his practice of eating and drinking with the despised of his time. By contrast, he is never cited for feats of asceticism, nor is his celibacy highlighted, either by himself or by his contemporaries. The focus is elsewhere on his love and service of people, flowing from his relationship with God.

3. **He Is the Sacrament of God's Presence, Love, and Power.** "Emmanuel" is what Matthew's Gospel calls Jesus, "God with us" (Mt 1:23). That is how people experience him. John's Gospel calls him "the Word," a term with a rich background in the Hebrew Scriptures. The Hebrew people knew God to be self-communicating, and everything they heard from God, whether in nature, in historical events, or in prophetic spokespersons, they called God's word. Applying this pregnant term to Jesus means that all God wants to communicate to humankind is gathered right here, in this man, not just in his words but in his whole personhood. It means that Jesus is a sacrament, for sacramentality is nothing else but making the invisible visible. "The person who sees me sees the Father" (Jn 14:9).

The most striking experience of God's gracious outreach in Jesus was his table fellowship with sinners. In this good man's acceptance of them, people experienced God's own acceptance, forgiveness, and affirmation. It gave them a new lease on life. This entire Gospel tradition of gracious hosting is the background of our Eucharist.

Jesus' outreach has other forms too, as in the calling of poor fishermen, talking at length with a woman drawing water, inviting Zacchaeus to come down from his tree and host him, raising the son of the widow of Naim, accepting the hospitality and friendship of Martha and Mary. The response of people to Jesus shows that in him they recognize the sacrament of God: present, loving, powerful against everything that blocks access to life.

It is in this sacramentality of his to others that the first two outstanding features of Jesus' life converge. He reaches out to others as an overflow of his union with God, who sends him to humanity out of the divine love. As Jesus serves people in a human way, they experience the God who fills him.

4. Jesus is Free. The personality of Jesus is original. He is his own person. His replies to questions are fresh, unexpected. His parables are ingenious. His responses to situations are always surprising, e.g., when he deals with the tax due to Caesar (Mk 12), with the woman who washes his feet with her tears (Lk 7), with the Pharisees' demand for a sign (Mk 8). The great bulk of his teaching is his own, showing fresh departures, winning admiration (Mt 7).

Jesus is free from other people's expectations. He will not accommodate Herod with a miracle even to save his life (Lk 23), will not let the people make him king (Jn 6), will not resort to violence though violence is used against him (Mt 26). His relatives come to take him away because they think he is mad (Mk 3). His own brothers do not believe in him (Jn 7). His disciples frequently show misunderstanding and disagreement, and Peter challenges him directly (Mk 8). But Jesus stays the course, even when it is a very lonely one.

He is free from the law and the tradition. He is respectful of both, and lives by and large within them. But he does not hesitate to set them aside when he sees a greater value. So he sets aside the Sabbath observance to help someone in need, sets aside capital punishment to save a woman caught in adultery, sets aside fasting in the interest of table fellowship. Many of Jesus' actions would be called civil disobedience today. His was a society in which religious law and civil law were one. So it was civil disobedience to touch a leper, to eat with tax collectors, to release an adulteress from the death penalty, to heal, or to take grain from the fields on the Sabbath, to exempt oneself from fasting laws. But Jesus lived a set of values which sometimes required civil disobedience.

Jesus was free from possessions. He was an itinerant preacher with no place to lay his head. He depended upon the hospitality of others. At his death, there was nothing to divide up except one garment.

Jesus was free from fear. He could not be bought. Not that he did not feel fear. He felt it keenly, but he would not be governed by it. He continued to do the good and to speak the truth in the face of every threat — of arrest, of calumny, of death. Threats availed nothing with him.

JESUS' TEACHING

We have looked at some of the outstanding features of Jesus' life. What did he teach? His life and teaching are of a piece. He teaches the same values that he lives.

1. **The Love of God.** God is for us. We can trust God, because God knows what we need before we ask (Mt 6). The very hairs of our heads are numbered (Mt 10). We can rely on God's love in spite of sin and failure because God is compassionate (Lk 6). Indeed, God's mercy is seen in action in the public ministry of Jesus, the image of God (2 Cor 5) who reaches out to sinners. God's will has a sovereign claim on us. It is summed up in Jesus' great commandment: love of God and love of neighbor (Mt 22). We love God because God has first loved us. Much of Jesus' teaching is directed to reimaging God for us as loving parent with all that follows from that understanding.

2. **Love of Neighbor.** Jesus lays great stress on our relationships with one another, and here too what he teaches is what he lives. Our love should extend to all, even to those who hate us, malign us, oppress or persecute us. We should pray for them, and do good to them (Mt 5). We should love the sinner. Jesus teaches us to forgive injuries after the model of God's forgiveness of our sins (Mt 18). We are supposed to forgive the same injury, even if it occurs again and again (Mt 18). Jesus teaches us to love the poor, even to the extent of selling all we have and giving it to them (Mk 10). His parable of the good Samaritan tells us to help those who need help, even if we do not know them, or if their path crosses our at a most inconvenient time (Lk 10). We should feed the hungry, give drink to the thirsty, welcome the stranger, clothe the naked, visit those who are ill or in prison (Mt 25). We should serve one another, even to washing one another's feet (Jn 13).

Jesus offers two different standards for measuring whether our love for others is what it should be. One is that we love others the way we love ourselves (Mt 22). The other is that we love one another the way Jesus loves us (Jn 13). The detail in which Jesus draws out this teaching makes it clear that he has something different from a general sentiment in mind. "I love humanity," Charlie Brown says. "It's people I can't stand." In Jesus' teaching, it is the neighbor, not humanity, who is to be loved, the person who is there in the flesh, not the abstraction.

3. **Simplicity of Life.** Jesus tells us not to lay up treasure for ourselves on earth (Mt 6). He insists that we cannot serve God and mammon (Mt 6). He calls the poor blessed and pronounces woes on the rich (Lk 6). In a paradigmatic encounter, he tells a rich young man that he should sell

all he has and follow him (Mk 10). He says that it is easier for a camel to get through the eye of a needle than for a rich person to enter God's kingdom (Mk 10). In a parable he depicts a man who is busy building himself bigger barns and calls him a fool (Lk 12). His parable of the rich man and poor Lazarus puts Lazarus in the bosom of Abraham and the rich man in Hades (Lk 16).

These are not Jesus' best loved teachings in the West today, where Christians enjoy affluence. It is hard to know how to live them. But it is impossible to deny or minimize them, given their frequency in the Gospels. Jesus talked about riches and poverty more than about almost any other subject, including heaven and hell, sex, divorce, Church authority, or the law. One out of every ten verses in the first three Gospels is about rich and poor, one out of seven in Luke. Even in the Hebrew Scriptures, this is the second most common theme, the first being the related theme of idolatry.

Why such centrality? Probably for two reasons. The first is that where our treasure is, our heart is, too (Mt 6). It is very hard to serve both God and mammon. The other is the plight of needy brothers and sisters, for whom God wants life also. Part of the contemporary realization is that giving a beggar a quarter does not sufficiently answer the commandment. This is how politics and economics have found their way into the pulpit against some people's objections. In a world in such dire economic imbalance, in which a small percentage of wealthy people enjoy so much while such masses of people struggle for bare existence and often lose the battle to disease or starvation, Jesus' teaching challenges the very structure of national and world economics. This situation is incompatible with the reign of God. Figuring out how to redistribute the goods of the earth in response to the love commandment is one of the great challenges of our day.

4. **An Attitude of Suffering**. Jesus' own efforts to ease people's burdens and his sending of his disciples to do the same indicates where he stands on the question of human suffering. His first response to it is to struggle against it, to eradicate or lessen it. And if we see in him what God is doing and wants done, then we also know where God stands on human suffering. God's cause is the human cause. God wants life for us, not death. Jesus points to the fruits of his labors as the sign that the reign of God is taking over: the blind see, the lame walk, lepers are cleansed, the dead are raised, and the poor have good news preached to them (Mt 11). What Jesus says of evil in the world, both as sin and as suffering, is that "an enemy has done this" (Mt 13:28). The exact identity of the enemy is difficult to construe, but it is clear from this parable of the wheat and the weeds that the master of the field sowed good seed, not weeds. And what this means for

our present purposes is that God labors with us, not against us, as we strive to overcome sin and suffering. So our first response to suffering is to resist and eradicate it. On this the whole healing ministry of the Church is based.

The second response to suffering comes only after we have done all we can to overcome it. It is to accept the unsolved remainder in hope. It is to trust in God, whose power goes beyond our own and often works secretly. Jesus himself resists death until he cannot anymore. He slips through the crowd that would throw him over the mountainside (Lk 4:30), and avoids being seen in public when his enemies are lying in wait (Jn 11:54). But when his hour comes, he accepts the suffering and death that come to him, placing his trust in God. Everything that Jesus teaches about trust in God in the face of life's difficulties grounds this second response to suffering: accept the unsolved remainder in hope.

There are two pitfalls into which Christian discipleship falls in this matter of suffering. One is to seek suffering for its own sake, as if it had the highest value. The other is to seek joy, trying to avoid all suffering. Both are mistakes. In the teaching of Jesus, suffering and joy are by-products, never the object of direct seeking. The object of direct seeking in the Gospel is to do the good, to live the truth, to love God and neighbor. If we dedicate our lives to these goals, we will suffer. And we will have joy. They are both accompaniments of Gospel living, as they were both accompaniments of Jesus' life. Jesus knows great suffering and deep joy, but he does not directly seek either. His eyes are fixed on other goals.

DISCIPLESHIP

When people begin to think about the spiritual life, which is another way of speaking of discipleship, somehow they lose their way. They forget the main emphases of the Gospel, and lapse into religiosity. The initial mistake may lie in speaking of "the spiritual life" in the first place. Jesus just talks about life.

Yet, somehow, when people think about practicing their faith more earnestly, they resolve on the following: they will meditate everyday, they will go more frequently to the Eucharist, they will seek sacramental reconciliation regularly, they will get themselves a spiritual director, they will join a prayer group, they will increase their devotions, they will undertake fasting or some other penance, they will do more spiritual reading, and they will talk religiously. This seems like a serious spiritual program, the way to follow Jesus, become holy, and get close to God.

I can think of a number of people I have known who have done all these things and yet do not really live the Gospel. They have never been converted though they are religiously very active and their talk is unmistakably religious. What are they missing?

To answer that question we have to take a look at what is really wrong with human beings, what stands in need of radical conversion. There are several things.

1. **We do not trust God.** We do not really believe that God loves us because there are too many things wrong with us. Not only do we not believe that we are accepted and even cherished for whom we are, but we do not trust in God's care for us either. We figure that we had better make provision for the morrow, or the morrow will surely destroy us. We are anxious about many things, quite sure they will not work out. We do not trust God.

2. **We do not like ourselves.** We beat on ourselves constantly. We put ourselves down. We screen out affirmation and nurse the remarks that hurt us. We compare ourselves unfavorably with others. We are well aware of all that is wrong with us and acknowledge almost none of our gifts. We withhold ourselves from others, figuring that we have nothing to offer, and that if we let them know us, they would most likely reject us. We have already rejected ourselves.

3. **We do not like other people.** Oh, we do like certain ones. But we do not like most of them. We don't like women, or we don't like men. We don't like Hispanics, or maybe it's blacks, Polacks, orientals, or Jews. We don't like commies, or queers, or hippies, or maybe we don't like straights or squares. Much of it is fear. We have never met one, and do not want to take the chance. We hang on to our grudges too, against aunts and uncles, parents, children, even those with whom we share bed and board. Thank God there are a few people we can love but sometimes they are hard to find.

4. **We seek happiness and security in wealth and power.** We want to be comfortable. We want to cut a successful figure in the world, to command respect. We want to grab all the gusto we can get, and be on easy street tomorrow. A good dog or two should be able to guard our possessions, backed up by a small handgun. Against larger numbers, some well-placed nuclear warheads should do the trick. To live is to have many things, and to be safe is to be fully insured and well defended.

In sum, we are selfish and prejudiced, hard-hearted and closed-minded. We are judgmental and unforgiving. And often we are sorry we are alive. We do not view life as a gift and an opportunity, but see it as a burden and a drag, complaining about how awful it is or how bored we are. These are the things that are wrong with us. These are the things that need to change.

Jesus offers to heal our diseases with his life, his teaching, and his gift of the Holy Spirit. The process requires our cooperation. Almost always in the Gospel, Jesus required the cooperation of the patient in a healing. They had to take up their bed and walk (Mk 2), go and show themselves to the priest (Lk 10), go and wash in the pool (Jn 9). The spiritual healing we all need entails a transformation of all our relationships: to God, to ourselves, to others, to things. The changing of our relationships changes us, for we are constituted the persons we are precisely by our relationships. But we have to cooperate with the Lord's action.

1. **He changes our relationship to God.** He puts us into a relationship of love with God. He teaches us that God is compassionate and merciful and accepts us as we are. He teaches and shows us that God can be trusted to take care of us.

2. **He changes our relationship to ourselves.** By his love and reverence for each person, even the most abandoned or unpromising, Jesus shows us that we are good. Are we any worse than the people in the Gospels? God's acceptance of us in Jesus becomes the basis for our self-acceptance. It is all right to be imperfect, limited, in process. It is all right to fall, if we are just willing to get up again.

3. **He changes our relationship to others.** He tells us to love, shows us how to do it, and gives us his Spirit to empower us. He teaches and models the path of reconciliation. He shows us that we find life and God not in isolation but in involvement, in our relationships with one another.

4. **He changes our relationship to things.** He teaches and models simplicity of life, the opposite of acquisitiveness, and tells us that if someone steals something from us we should give that person more besides (Mt 5:38-42). Not only does he teach this sort of *freedom* from things; he teaches us a *contemplative attitude* toward them as well. All of his teachings are derived from the ordinary things of the world — seed and harvest, the seasons, children, banquets and weddings, birds and lilies, sheep and shepherds. In all things Jesus sees the creative and generous hand of God, and in nature he reads the parables of God. If he can see these things, perhaps we can learn to see them too.

This is how we are healed, through this transformation of all our relationships, which brings with it the transformation of ourselves. This is Christian discipleship and Christian spirituality. It is also salvation, at least the first installment on it.

What is the relationship between these demanding transformations of our selfhood and the religious practices we enumerated earlier — the meditation, sacraments, prayer group, etc.? They sustain the Christian life. It is

very difficult to keep Christian values in focus, and to live the demands of
discipleship if we do not read Scripture, pray, and lean on other Christians
for support and direction. The culture does not encourage us. We need
reminders, symbols, stories, exhortations, living models, times out for
reflection, and times for celebration. These things are indispensable sup-
ports. The error is to think that these things *are* the Christian life. Just as
Jesus' practice of prayer was in the service of his whole way of life, a
means rather than an end, so must ours be. It was his whole life that was
his worship of God. So must ours be. Insofar as prayer, sacraments, reading, and spiritual direction support genuine Christian living, i.e., Christian
attitudes, relationships, choices, and action, they are useful. When they
become an escape from the more difficult demands of Christian living, they
are the corruption of discipleship. The question at the last judgment is not
"How religious was your talk?" nor "How much time did you spend in
prayer?" nor "Was your faith orthodox in every respect?" It is, rather,
"How did you respond to needy brothers and sisters?" (Mt 25). That is one
reliable measure of our discipleship. Paul offers a more elaborate set of cri-
teria: charity, joy, peace, patience, mildness, generosity, long-suffering, and
self-control (Gal 5:22-23).

FRIENDSHIP WITH JESUS CHRIST

Jesus is not just a teacher, nor just a model for us to imitate. Jesus
still lives, and he offers himself to each of us as companion and friend.
This is a very important aspect of Christian discipleship, and the New
Testament lays a great deal of stress on it.

And know that I am with you always, even till the end of the
world (Mt 28:20).

Anyone who lives me will be true to my word, and my Father
will love him; we will come to him and make our dwelling
place with him (Jn 14:23).

Here I stand, knocking at the door. If anyone hears me calling
and opens the door, I will enter his house, and dine with him
(Rev 3:20).

No longer do I call you servants; I have called you friends (Jn
15:15).

This personal relationship with Christ is a very attractive and com-
forting aspect of Christian spirituality. It takes some of the work out of it. It
gives one a companion and friend in all seasons, all circumstances. Such
friendship is different from ordinary human friendships in that this friend is

not visible or tangible. He is also a more exalted friend, God with us. Yet a genuine friendship with him is possible, because he is present to us, is interested in us, and does want to share with us. These are the essential ingredients of a friendship.

St. Paul's whole life is based on his friendship with Jesus Christ. We see the same thing in many of the later saints. Paul says, "For me, to live is Christ" (Phil 1:21). Paul turns his whole life over to Christ, trusts him, thinks about him, praises him, asks him for what he needs, conceives all his lifework in terms of Christ, and gratefully receives the constant love of Christ. "He loved me and gave himself up for me" (Gal 2:20). This is the idea. Paul's oft repeated expression for the Christian life is life "in Christ." He is a fine example of that kind of living Jesus speaks of in his farewell discourse.

> I am the vine; you are the branches. The person who lives in me
> and I in him will produce abundantly, for apart from me you can
> do nothing (Jn 15:5).

Paul puts it this way: "I can do all things in him who strengthens me" (Phil 4:13).

All of us need this kind of resource, and it is offered to us. What do we have to do to establish this relationship? Nothing more than ask for it, and open our hearts to receive it. But we must seriously want Christ in our lives. We have to be willing to turn our lives over to him in trust and obedience, imitating the way he turned his life over in trust and obedience to his Father. The friendship we are speaking of here is not given once and for all. Like all other friendships, it is a living reality. It requires tending or it dies. But if it is tended through the exercise of sharing, of giving and receiving in all those ways that Paul, for example, exercised it, then it grows, and we ourselves grow increasingly into the image of Christ. Ephesians sums it up in the form of prayer.

> May Christ dwell in your hearts through faith, and may charity
> be the root and foundation of your life. Thus you will be able to
> grasp fully, with all the saints, the breadth and length and height
> and depth of Christ's love, and experience this love which sur-
> passes all knowledge, so that you may attain to all the fullness
> of God (Eph 3:17-19).

HOW I GROW

1. The most important insights I learned about Jesus and discipleship...

_____
_____
_____
_____
_____
_____
_____
_____
_____
_____
_____

2. Ways I can use these insights in my life and in my ministry...

_____
_____
_____
_____
_____
_____
_____
_____
_____
_____

3. Questions I need to explore in future learning:

_____
_____
_____
_____
_____
_____
_____
_____
_____
_____
_____

5

CHURCH AND MINISTRY

WHERE I STAND

1. For me, Church means...

2. An image of the Church that is appealing to me...

3. The mission of the Church is to...

4. For me, Christian ministry means...

5. I feel called to Christian ministry because...

6. The most difficult thing about my ministry...

READING   RICHARD McBRIEN

Ministry is difficult to define and individual ministries are difficult to distinguish from each other because ministry's origin and history are very complex. But there are some constants, one of which is that ministry is for the sake of the Church's mission. To understand Christian ministry (in its universal and specific meanings) one must see it always in relation to the nature and mission of the Church.

First, what do we mean by Church? Is the Church the hierarchy (pope and bishops) or it is the whole People of God? Is it the institution or is it the community? It's both, as a matter of fact.

Is the Church a parish, a diocese, or a base community, or is it universal and centered, for Catholics, in the Vatican? Is the Church local or is it international? Again, it's both. Finally, is the Church Catholic or Protestant? Is it Anglican or Orthodox? Is it denominational or ecumenical? One more time: it's both.

The word *Church* admits of many different, but not contradictory, meanings. Its root meaning is *assembly*. For our purposes here I define the Church as the whole community (assembly) of baptized persons called by God the Father to acknowledge the lordship of Jesus, the Son of God, in word, in worship, in witness, and in service and, through the power of the Holy Spirit, to share in Jesus' historic mission for the sake of the Kingdom of God. In short, the Church is the Body of Christ.

THE MISSION OF THE CHURCH

The Church is first called and then *sent*. In other words, the Church is a community, or an assembly, with a *mission*. The mission of the Church is similar to that of Jesus Christ himself. Like Christ, the Church "receives the mission to proclaim and to establish among all peoples the kingdom of Christ and of God" (*Dogmatic Constitution on the Church*, n. 5).

First, the Church is sent to proclaim the Kingdom of God by *word*, that is, in preaching, teaching, and catechesis. Second, the Church is sent to participate in Christ's *worship* of the Father, in and through the power of the Holy Spirit. The Church does this especially in the Eucharist, which Vatican II called the summit and the source of the whole Christian life (*Constitution on the Sacred Liturgy*, n. 10) and which anticipates the feasting we hope to enjoy in the heavenly kingdom. The Church also celebrates and anticipates the coming kingdom in the other sacraments and in its general prayer life.

Third, the Church is sent to offer *witness* to the world of what it proclaims and celebrates. Because the Church is a sacrament — as Pope Paul VI said, a "reality imbued with the hidden presence of God" — it has to practice what it preaches. It is not enough that it *be* the Body of Christ; it must *look* and *act* like the Body of Christ. It is not enough that it *be* "the initial budding forth of the kingdom" (*Dogmatic Constitution on the Church*, n. 5); it must *look* and *act* like a community permeated with God's saving presence.

Finally, the Church is sent to provide *service* to those in need, both inside and outside the Church. In this regard it must follow the example of the Lord himself who, as the Suffering Servant of God, ministered to the sick, the poor, the handicapped, the oppressed, the socially ostracized, the sinners, and the dying. The Kingdom of God, after all, is a kingdom of justice and peace, as well as of holiness and grace.

Ministry is exercised, therefore, across the whole missionary spectrum. Thus there are ministries of the word (catechist, preacher), ministries of worship (choir director, eucharistic minister, lector, presider), ministries of witness (those that serve the ongoing renewal and reform of religious communities, of local churches, or of the universal Church), and ministries of service (social ministries of various kinds, such as to the elderly, handicapped, sick, and refugees).

Because the mission of the Church is not limited to liturgy, for example, there are more authentic, designated ministries than those related directly to the Eucharist and the other sacraments. And because service (*diakonia*) is part of the essential mission of the Church, ministries that serve the handicapped, the poor, and the politically oppressed are as authentic as ministries of preaching, teaching, and catechesis.

THE KINGDOM OF GOD

According to Vatican II, "the Church has a single intention: that God's kingdom may come" (*Pastoral Constitution on the Church in the Modern World*, n. 45). This is not surprising since the Church is the Body of Christ, and the Kingdom of God was at the very center of Jesus' own mission: "This is the time of fulfillment. The Kingdom of God is at hand. Repent and believe in the gospel" (Mk 1:15).

The Kingdom of God, however, is harder to define than is the Church. You can see the Church; you can't see the Kingdom. Although the Christian believes that God is present and active in the Church, there is more to the Church than its divine and supernatural character. There is a human and worldly dimension that is within the reach, so to speak, of social scientist and other interested observers. People identify themselves and are identified by others as members of the Church. The Church has a membership list, owns property, has employees, registers with the government for tax purposes, and the like.

Accordingly, a sociologist can analyze the Church, examining its methods of recruitment, formation, and guidance, noting how power is distributed and exercised, measuring its stated goals against its palpable achievements. But a sociologist cannot analyze the Kingdom of God. The Kingdom of God isn't an organization, an institution, or a social movement. People don't "join" the Kingdom. The Kingdom doesn't own property, nor does it have any employees.

This is not to suggest that there is something unreal or abstract about the Kingdom. Whatever the Church is and does, it always acts for the sake of the Kingdom of God.

What, then, is the Kingdom of God? A *kingdom* is a territory or region under a particular person's control. Thus we have the Hashemite Kingdom of Jordan, under the control of the King of Jordan. His will determines social, economic, and political policy in Jordan. What happens in Jordan ultimately depends on the will of its king.

But *kingdom* can also describe the territory or region in a different, nonpolitical sense. A person is hired as a new secretary in a large corporation. As she begins her first day on the job, some of the other secretaries help to familiarize her not only with her duties but also with the politics of the office. "That one over there, the woman with the red blouse. She's a great person. You'd never know she's the comptroller. Very down-to-earth." Then the finger points in another direction. "But don't stick your nose over there. That's the executive vice-president's secretary. She runs that operation like a staff sergeant. That's her kingdom, and you'd better not forget it."

The Kingdom of God is more like the second that the first, but without the negative overtones. The Kingdom exists wherever and whenever the will of God is operative, wherever and whenever the will of God is fulfilled.

The Kingdom of God is as broad and as overarching as the will of God is broad and overarching. In God, of course, everything is one. God is not separate from the will of God. If the Kingdom of God is the will of God in force, then the Kingdom of God *is* God. More precisely the Kingdom of God is God insofar as God is redemptively present and active in the human heart, in the midst of a group of people, in a community, in institutions and movements, in the world at large, in nature, in the cosmos.

The Kingdom of God is a past, present, and future reality, since God is past, present, and future all at once. The Kingdom of God has already broken into history. We see reference after reference to it in the Old Testament. The Kingdom of God is a present reality — our God is a living God, and the will of God is being fulfilled even now. Finally, the Kingdom of God is a coming, or future, reality. Indeed the Lord taught us to pray: "Thy Kingdom come, thy will be done..."

How does the Kingdom come about? First, it is always the Kingdom of *God*. God, not humans, brings about the Kingdom. On the other hand, God invites and requires human collaboration in the realization of the

Kingdom. We are co-workers with God in the coming of God's final reign over all creation.

TOWARD A DEFINITION OF MINISTRY

Although there are different approaches to ministry in recent theological writings and ecumenical documents, certain important points have been agreed upon: 1) ministry is rooted in the Holy Spirit; 2) there is a distinction between general and particular ministry; 3) all ministry is functional; that is, for the benefit of others, not primarily for the benefit of the minister; and 4) ultimately all ministry is for the sake of the Kingdom of God which is the object of the Church's mission.

There are four levels of ministry:

1. General/universal ministry is any service (which is the root meaning of the word *ministry*) rendered to another person or group of people who happen to be in need of that service. The call to ministry in this first sense is rooted in our common humanity. In other words, every human being is called to general/universal ministry. In this sense ministry has nothing intrinsically to do with religion. Examples of this ministry include taking care of a single parent's children, shopping for an elderly neighbor, demonstrating against nuclear weapons, or contributing to a fund for starving people.

2. General/specific ministry is any special service rendered by people specifically called to serve others in the so-called helping professions and other service occupations such as nursing, social work, and legal aid. Their ministry is rooted not only in their humanity but also in a particular competence that is publicly certified or validated in one way or another, such as by licensing.

3. Christian/universal ministry is any general service rendered to others in Christ and because of Christ. The call to ministry in this third sense is rooted in our Baptism and Confirmation. Accordingly every member of the Church is called to ministry in this sense. And, in fact, when Christians perform the services in general/universal ministry, their actions are Christian/universal if performed out of explicitly Christian motives.

4. Christian/specific ministry is any special service rendered to others in Christ and because of Christ in the name of the Church and for the sake of helping the Church fulfill its mission. The call to ministry in this fourth and most specific sense is rooted in some form or act of designation by the Church itself. Thus, it is sometimes called designated ministry. Relatively few members of the Church are called to ministry in this sense.

A Christian who visits the sick on his or her own initiative is engaging in Christian/universal ministry. A Christian who visits the sick as part of a parish team that has been designated for this service is engaging in Christian/specific ministry. Other examples of Christian/specific ministers include directors of religious education, eucharistic ministers, lectors, ministers of hospitality, deacons, and, of course, bishops and presbyters.

With the declining numbers of vocations to the ordained priesthood in recent years, this ministerial category has expanded to include many lay people who were at one time excluded from meaningful participating in the liturgical, educational, administrative, and social ministries of the Church. But even if there had been no shortage of presbyteral vocations, this expansion would have occurred as a result of the Second Vatican Council's emphasis on the Church as the People of God (*Dogmatic Constitution on the Church*, ch. 2) and on Baptism and Confirmation as the sacramental foundation of Christian mission (*Dogmatic Constitution on the Church*, n. 33).

Of course, what ultimately grounds each of these four levels of ministry is the gracious action of the Holy Spirit. Each of us, Christian or not, ordained or not, is empowered by God, the author and source of all life and of all gifts, to do good for others, that is, to render unselfish service to our neighbors. This empowering, charism-bestowing God is called the Holy Spirit.

In turn, every level of ministry is oriented to the same reality — namely, the coming Kingdom of God, a kingdom not only of holiness and grace, but of justice, love, and peace.

READING   CATHOLIC BISHOPS OF THE UNITED STATES

THE CALL TO MINISTRY

From the reception of these charisms or gifts, including those which are less dramatic, there arises for each believer the right and duty to use them in the Church and the world for the good of humankind and for the upbuilding of the Church. (*Decree on the Apostolate of the Laity*, n.3).

Baptism and Confirmation empower all believers to share in some form of ministry. Although the specific form of participation in ministry varies according to the gifts of the Holy Spirit, all who share in this work are united with one another. "Just as each of us has one body with many members, and not all the members have the same function, so too we, though many, are one body in Christ and individually members of one another. We have gifts that differ according to the favor bestowed on each of us" (Rom 12:4-6).

CHRISTIAN SERVICE: MINISTRY IN THE WORLD

> The laity, by their vocation, seek the Kingdom of God by engaging in temporal affairs, and by ordering them according to the plan of God (*Lumen Gentium*, n. 31).

Christian service in the world is represented in a pre-eminent way by the laity. It is sometimes called the "ministry of the laity" and balances the concept of ministry found in the Church. Ministry, broadly understood includes civic and public activity, response to the imperatives of peace and justice, and resolution of social, political, and economic conflicts, especially as they influence the poor, oppressed and minorities.

The whole Church faces unprecedented situations in the contemporary world, and lay people are at the cutting edge of these new challenges. It is they who engage directly in the task of relating Christian values and practices to complex questions such as business ethics, political choice, economic security, quality of life, cultural development and family planning.

Really new situations, especially in the realm of social justice, call for creative responses. We know that the Spirit moves among all the People of God, prompting them according to their particular gifts and offices, to discern anew the signs of the times and to interpret them boldly in light of the Gospel. Lay women and men are in a unique position to offer this service.

MINISTRY IN THE CHURCH

> As sharers in the role of Christ the Priest, the Prophet, and the King, the laity have an active part to play in the life and activity of the Church (*Decree on the Apostolate of the Laity*, n. 10).

Since the Second Vatican Council new opportunities have developed for lay men and women to serve in the Church. We acknowledge gratefully the continuing and increasing contributions of volunteers and part time workers who serve on parish and diocesan councils, boards of education, and financial, liturgical, and ecumenical committees, as well as those who exercise roles such as special minister of the Eucharist, catechist, and pastoral assistant. We are grateful, too, for the large numbers of lay people who have volunteered and are serving in the missions.

Growing numbers of lay women and men are also preparing themselves professionally to work in the Church. In this regard religious sisters and brothers have shown the way with their initiative and creativity.

Ecclesial ministers, i.e. lay persons who have prepared for professional ministry in the Church, represent a new development. We welcome this as a gift to the Church. There are also persons who serve the Church by the witness of their lives and their self-sacrificing service and empowerment of the poor in works such as administration, housing, job development, and education. All these lay ministers are undertaking roles which are not yet clearly spelled out and which are already demanding sacrifices and risks of them and their families. As lay persons increasingly engage in ecclesial ministry, we recognize and accept the responsibility of working out practical difficulties such as the availability of positions, the number of qualified applicants, procedures for hiring, just wages, and benefits.

The combination of all these responses to the challenges of our time proclaims the interrelated oneness of ministry as a gift of the Spirit, and we rejoice in this.

Called and Gifted: The American Catholic Laity (Excerpts).

HOW I GROW

1. The most important insights I learned about Church and Ministry...

_____
_____
_____
_____
_____
_____

2. Ways I can use these insights in my life and in my ministry...

_____
_____
_____
_____
_____

3. Questions I need to explore in future learning:

_____
_____
_____
_____
_____
_____

6

THE
SACRAMENTS

WHERE I STAND

1. Times that I have specially experienced God's presence...

2. For me, a symbol is...

3. A sacramental symbol that is special or significant to me...

4. For me, sacraments are...

5. The sacramental celebration which touched me most deeply was...

6. The sacraments are important in my life as a Christian because...

ESSAY   SANDRA DeGIDIO, OSM

I once asked a group of parents during a talk if they remembered the definition of a sacrament from the *Baltimore Catechism*. A father, who was obviously not happy about being at the talk, growled from his slouched position in the back row: "A sacrament is an outward sign instituted by Christ to give grace."

"Right," I responded, "and it's really not a bad definition."

"It was good enough for Baltimore," he shot back, "and it's good enough for me!"

Indeed, it was good enough for the 19th century. And beyond that, it is still a definition that works fairly well today. It just doesn't go quite far enough.

The definition actually originated not with the Council of Baltimore in 1884, which produced the *Baltimore Catechism*, but with St. Augustine in the fifth century. He said that a sacrament was "a visible sign of invisible grace." From Augustine, the phrase filtered down to be used through the Middle Ages, the Council of Trent and scholastic theology. Each age elaborated on it and viewed it through its own theological perspective.

Today, with our renewed theology and reformed liturgical rites we have come to see sacraments in a much broader sense than the catechism definition might suggest. Actually, we have come to see sacraments more in the sense that St. Augustine saw them.

Sacraments are more than seven ritual acts that give grace. Rather, they are opportunities for people already in God's grace to gather and celebrate that fact through symbolic action or ritual. Our understanding of sacraments today begins not with church rituals, but with the experience of God's presence and care in our daily life.

Sacraments don't happen in church so much as they happen in people who come together as *Church* to celebrate what has already been happening in them. Sacraments are *lived* long before they are celebrated.

For example, many people may have a strong, "living" sense of God's loving and nourishing presence apart from sharing that presence in the Eucharist, or even before they are baptized. But when they share Christ's Body in the Eucharist, they "realize" and celebrate this presence in a special way. Even in the case of infant Baptism, the Church celebrates at the time of Baptism the overflowing love that God has for that child from the time it was born. Thus, in a true sense, the sacraments are signs of what is happening between God and us 24 hours a day but which is ritualized and *made real* in a special manner when the sacraments is celebrated liturgically.

THE BROADER PERSPECTIVE OF SACRAMENTS

To understand how this can be, we must broaden our concept of sacrament, and make a distinction between sacrament in general and the Church's seven ritual sacraments.

A sacrament in the broadest sense can be any person, event, or thing through which we encounter or experience God's presence in a new or deeper way. A sunset, a period of quiet prayer, a storm, the birth of a child, an intimate conversation with a close friend can all have the potential for revealing God to us in new and deeper ways.

The phrase *potential for* is important here. Such experiences may not always be sacramental for all people. Some aspects of creation are more "charged" with God than others. And also, people vary in their capacity to see God in these broad sacramental manifestations. For example, a sunset or a conversation with a close friend is a better sacramental experience for me than a storm or the birth of a child. (Storms frighten me, and I have never experienced a birth.)

This broad concept of sacraments is really not new. The Old Testament is full of such sacramental events touching the lives of the Hebrew people long before the Church defined or categorized sacraments. For the Hebrews, the dove returning the Noah carrying an olive branch, the flood, the miracles of the prophets, Creation, the parting of the Red Sea all had very sacramental dimensions. The Exodus (the escape of the Israelites from slavery in Egypt under the leadership of Moses) was definitely a sacramental experience. In their journey through the desert from slavery to freedom, they found water from rocks and bread from heaven, and they discovered that Yahweh was indeed loving, powerful and intimately concerned with their welfare. Through the Exodus event, the Israelites came to recognize Yahweh in an entirely new way, and their whole history was altered. As a result, they told and retold the story, not just in words but in symbols and actions through their Passover ritual.

In the broad sense, then, we can say that a sacramental experience is an encounter with God which somehow changes us. Virtually any human experience can provide us with such an encounter.

CHRISTIAN SACRAMENTS

The Church's ritual sacraments have their roots in this broad idea of sacraments. The Christian sacraments we know today originated with a human experience, an experience of people who were followers of Jesus. By experiencing the person of Jesus, those people encountered God and God's presence in a new way. Indeed, Jesus was for them the sacrament of God. The encounter with Jesus changed them, and they shared the story of that transformation like the Hebrew people—not just with words and narratives but with symbolic actions.

They told the story of Jesus, but they also lived the story. Like Jesus, they went into the waters of Baptism to symbolize their new life. They broke bread and shared it as a symbol of God's love and care for them and their love and care for each other. They prayed for each other, laid hands on each other, healed and forgave — just as they had seen Jesus break bread, pray for, lay hands on, heal and forgive. As Jesus was the sacrament of God for them, they, the Church, became the sacrament of Jesus.

Thus the Church's sacraments were born, even though they may not yet have been enumerated or named. Out of that birth came the beginning of the definition with which most of us grew up.

THE SACRAMENTS AS SYMBOLS

Let's look more closely at that definition, phrase by phrase. At the same time we can accept it as a valid definition, we realize that it needs expansion.

"A sacrament is an outward sign" — true, Christian sacraments are signs. However, our theology of sacraments assumes a meaning if the sacraments are seen as *symbols*, which means they are more than simply "outward signs." A sign carries a single meaning which has been arbitrarily assigned to it. For example, a stop sign has one single informative meaning. Symbols have multiple meanings. They convey more than information. Symbols bring us into touch with the familiar and the mysterious simultaneously.

A wedding ring is a symbol of such multilayered meaning. At its most basic level it is a sign that the person wearing it is not a single person. But its meaning doesn't stop there. It has deeper meaning and special memories for the person wearing it, as well as for the person who gave it. In addition, it has different meanings and evokes memories for the person who sees it. At the same time, it is symbolic of the mystery of love between two people who become symbols for others of the mystery of the eternal love of God for people.

Similarly, the waters of Baptism symbolize life and death, washing and cleansing, and the mystery of new life out of death. The bread and wine of Eucharist are symbolic of God's care, nourishment, love, nurturance and sacrifice for us; and of our care, sharing, love, nurturance, nourishment and sacrifice for one another.

In a very real sense, the symbols which are the heart of the Church's sacraments are not primarily objects but actions. The symbols of the sacraments are all expressions of human intimacy — a bath, a meal, an embrace, a laying on of hands, a touch, a rubbing with oil. They do for us what words alone or abstract thought cannot do. They put the coming of God in our lives into body language. The symbolic acts at the heart of the sacraments help us break open and share with one another the common human experiences which reveal God's presence to us.

HOW THE SACRAMENTS ARE 'INSTITUTED BY CHRIST'

And what of that phrase "instituted by Christ"? I can remember as a child having a visual image of Jesus "instituting" the sacraments. As he walked along with his disciples, in my imagination, he would periodically stop, hold up his hand, two fingers raised, as he is so often depicted, and say, "Aha, I'll call it Confirmation...Matrimony...Baptism...and the outward signs will be oil...rings...water..." Of course, we are all older now and know that the phrase "instituted by Christ" is not best understood by imagining that Jesus had seven good ideas to which he gave names, as my childhood fancy might suggest. To picture Jesus thinking up the sacraments out of thin air, as it were, is hardly the way to understand their institution.

The sacraments, as we have said, arise out of the story of Jesus' life and actions, and as such are re-presentations of that life and of those actions. Jesus allowed himself to be baptized; he broke bread and shared it, thus sharing himself. Out of those special events in Jesus' life come our sacraments of Baptism and Eucharist. But the sacraments also flow from the very meaning of Jesus' life, from his values and teachings. He saw very basic values and experiences (forgiveness, concern for the sick, marriage, service) and he raised those values and experiences to new levels. He transformed those ordinary human values into spiritual values by helping people see God's love made visible through their living of those values.

Thus, while the sacraments were not necessarily thought up by Jesus, they were instituted by him because, clearly, they come from him. They come not only from his actions, but they strongly reflect his basic beliefs, values and teachings. What we celebrate as sacraments today, Jesus lived and gave special meaning to 2000 years ago.

As we celebrate the sacraments, we, like the first followers of Jesus, have the opportunity to encounter him precisely in our living of those same values which he lived and affirmed. In that encounter, Jesus is present to us as he was present to the early Church. In him we encounter God and God's presence. Jesus is the one great sacrament through which all other sacraments make sense.

THE SACRAMENTS AND THE 'GIVING OF GRACE'

This brings us to the final phrase of our definition: " ...to give grace." Many of us, I suspect, grew up with the notion that the sacraments provided us with a *thing* called grace which we were somehow lacking. But grace is not a *thing*, it is not a quantity that can be measured; it is a quality which defies measurement. Grace is essentially the gift of God's love and presence into which we grow. It is a relationship between God and us. Our side of the relationship develops gradually, but it is always a response to a love which was really always there.

The gift of God's grace is totally free and ever present. What we do with that gift is ours to choose. As with any gift, the gift of grace is ours to accept or reject. Our recognition that we have accepted it in our lives is what we celebrate in the sacraments.

The sacraments proclaim and enable us to express our response to that grace in our lives in word and symbolic action. The grace does not exist because we celebrate the sacraments; we celebrate the sacraments because the grace exists and we have responded to it. Sacraments do not provide, or bring into being, something which is otherwise absent. Rather, they celebrate God's grace which is already present long before we recognize or come to celebrate it.

The new sacramental rites are very clear about this. For example, the new Rite of Penance describes sacramental absolution as the "completion of the process of conversion." We used to say, "Go to confession and get forgiveness." The new rite says, in effect, "Experience the Lord's forgiveness in the community, then go to confession and celebrate the fact of that forgiveness."

Similarly, Baptism does not bring God's love into being. Baptism celebrates a family's and community's experience of that love in the baptized. There is, of course, a *deepening* of that love. The same is true of the Eucharist. Although we are already united to God and to others, our celebration of the Eucharist deepens, strengthens, renews and helps us "realize" this relationship even more.

Sacraments are lived before they are celebrated. They are, indeed, the "visible expressions of invisible grace" which St. Augustine defined. We celebrate sacraments because we recognize that gift of grace in ourselves, not merely to procure the gift. And yet, at the same time, we can certainly experience an *increase* or deepening of God's gift of grace in and though our celebration of the sacraments if we are open and receptive to it. That is why we say that the sacraments effect what they signify. They can and do effect a change in us if we are ready to accept that change. The marvelous mystery of God's grace is that, while it is always there awaiting our recognition and ritualization of it in our lives, in that very recognition and celebration the gift becomes even more present to us.

THE SACRAMENTS AND CHRISTIAN COMMUNITY

The grace of the sacraments can only be spoken of in *relational* terms. The new sacramental rites repeatedly speak of how the sacraments effect a deeper "relationship" or greater "conformity" with Christ and also with the Church.

This deepened relationship with Christ in the Church is an important aspect of sacraments which can be lost if we don't look beyond our cate-chism definition. Sacraments do not happen only to the individual. Sacraments can be understood completely only in relation to the Body of Christ which is the Church. St. Paul's metaphor of the Church as a body made up of many parts is significant in terms of our understanding of sacra-ments. Remember, Christian sacraments grew out of an experience of the living Christ by his followers who shared that experience in word and deed. Today Christ lives in us, the Church. He is experienced when the Christian community lives his values and celebrates the lived reality of his presence among us.

Sacraments, then, happen not simply to individuals, but to Christ's Body, the Church. When something happens to the Church (to paraphrase St. Paul) it happens to the individual. This is why the new rites insist that the sacraments be celebrated in the Christian assembly, with the community present and actively participating. The sacramental symbols are communal symbols which touch us as members of a community. The richness and effectiveness of the symbolism often depends on our degree of participation and responsiveness. The grace of the sacraments is the grace of the Church in service to others.

The gift of grace is there because of God's magnanimous love for us. We have only to experience it, celebrate it as sacrament and then go forth to *be* sacrament to the world — *be* that visible expression of God's love and care. We, like the first followers of Jesus, break bread and share it, pray for each other, lay hands on one another in love, heal and forgive. In so doing, we help strengthen the Christian community and offer a model for the building up of the whole human family.

SYMBOLS OF GOD'S CARE

Sacraments neither begin nor end with liturgical celebration. They begin with God's love and care through Christ to us, the Church. They con-tinue with us, the Church, living and enacting God's love and care through Christ to the world. In a real sense, they don't end. So long as we, the Church, continue to live and celebrate them, they are ongoing symbols of

God's care for all of us.

Yes, sacraments are "visible signs of invisible grace." They are "outward signs instituted by Christ to give grace"—and yet, they are ever so much more.

HOW I GROW

1. The most important insights I learned about the sacraments...

_____

_____

_____

_____

_____

_____

_____

_____

_____

_____

2. Ways I can use these insights in my life and in my ministry...

_____

_____

_____

_____

_____

_____

_____

_____

3. Questions I need to explore in future learning:

_____

_____

_____

_____

_____

_____

_____

_____

_____

_____

7

MORAL
DECISION-MAKING

WHERE I STAND

1. The most difficult thing about making moral decisions is...

2. When I make a moral decision, I usually consult...

3. I believe my conscience is important in making a moral decision because...

4. The Scriptures and Church teachings are important in making a moral decision because...

5. I believe it is acceptable to disagree with Church teachings when...

READING   NICHOLAS LOHKAMP, OFM

Many Catholics get dizzy when they see disagreement in the Church over such moral issues as birth control, divorce, the changing role of women or nuclear disarmament. How are we supposed to deal with the confusing relationship between personal conscience and official Church teaching?

Public disagreement with Church teaching on contraception, for example, is disturbing to many Catholics. Further disturbance arises when theologians publicly disagree with official Church teaching and, in general, urge greater freedom of conscience.

Why should there be ambiguity and confusion? How do we cope with it or live with it — or even come to understand it? How can all of us in the Church work together to understand and apply gospel values to our decisions? This essay hopes to answer these questions and shed some light on the complex link between our personal consciences and Church teaching.

A DIFFERENCE IN APPROACH

In the beginning we must realize that there is an important difference between gospel values themselves (the *content* of Church teaching) and the way they are proclaimed (the *method* of Church teaching). A major reason for confusion today is that we are in a transitional period, caught in a clash between two competing *methods* of arriving at moral principles: the "classical" and the "personal." These two methods are not contradictory, but they are very different. They are based on different ways of looking at reality.

1) The Classical Method. The goal of the classical or nonhistorical method is to capture what is universally true — for all people, all times, all circumstances. From the concrete and complex circumstances of everyday life, it deliberately abstracts — or draws forth, to use a less philosophical term — the *nature* or *essence* of the matter.

In the area of truthfulness, for example, this method would consider primarily the truth or falsity of statements. To a captured soldier trying to protect his comrades while undergoing questioning, it would say he could remain silent or rely on double-meaning statements. In the classical approach, he could not deliberately give false information; that would be telling a lie, which by its nature is always evil. Similarly, the classical method comes up with basic, unchangeable principles of sexual morality by carefully pondering the sexual nature of man and woman and the obvious relationship between the genital organs and reproduction.

The strength of this method is that it gives us valid insights into human nature expressed in logical, clear, precise terms. Its formulations can be addressed to all cultures in all times. It clearly avoids any danger of subjectivism.

The weakness of the classical method is that it too readily states in absolute terms the evil of certain concrete behavior without considering the persons involved, their situation, the changing aspects of history. It tends to underplay personal growth, relationships, the impact of cultural, social, economic and psychological factors. It can give the impression that official teachers always have absolute answers even when the questions are new and complex (such as bioethical issues dealing with test-tube babies and other matters undreamed of in medical practice a generation ago) and do not need to consult the expertise of laypersons or theologians.

The classical approach is still the method generally used by the Vatican. It was in keeping with the world view and language of many institutions and fields a century or two ago; it was at that time the logical method for the Church to use. Today, however, only those trained in scholastic philosophy and theology (which now excludes many priests) fully appreciate this method; the vast majority of Catholics do not understand the classical approach. Catholics get all tripped up in flatly rejecting such a *method*, because in so doing they may reject the *content* of Church teaching as well. (For example, they may wrongly see the Church as having nothing worthwhile to say about sexuality.) In the long run, this is disastrous.

2) The Personal Approach. The personal or historical approach starts by examining the experience of individuals. It traces the development of an idea or teaching through the years instead of focusing on human nature in the abstract. Its moral judgments consider the unique qualities and total personality of each individual, as well as how a person relates to others and to the community. From the practice of Christians down through the centuries and from the reflection, analysis and broad consultation, the personal approach seeks to formulate values and disvalues into universal laws.

The personal approach would thus say the captured soldier could give false information to the enemy because the value of truthfulness is outweighed by the value of saving other lives. In the matter of sexuality this method would consider the total persons involved, the meaning of love, and the experience of conscientious married couples.

The personal approach is the method used by the majority of theologians today as well as by most ordinary Catholics. Its relationship to personal human experience makes its positions seem reasonable — a stronger appeal in an age of democratic ideals rather than insistence on authority — even though the two methods often lead to the same conclusion.

THE INFALLIBLE IMPRESSION

A second reason for today's confusion is what I call the "infallible impression" — the tendency to assume noninfallible teaching is beyond disagreement.

The Church defines doctrine only on rare occasions: when the pope speaks *ex cathedra* or when an ecumenical council defines something as a matter of faith. The dogmas of the Immaculate Conception and the Assumption of Mary were infallible papal teachings; they defined matters essential to the Catholic faith. But Church authority (pope and bishops) also

teaches in *non*infallible ways — through encyclicals, pastoral statements
and the documents of national bishops' conferences, for instance.

Such teaching is important, but it is not infallible. It is presumed to
be true. Yet, in the course of history, many such teachings were changed. It
is misleading to leave the impression that such teaching is infallible and
that no one in good may faith withhold assent.

THE WORK OF THE SPIRIT

A third reason for present-day confusion is a tendency to over-sim-
plify the activity of the Holy Spirit. We trust the promise that the Spirit will
guide the Church, but we cannot overlook the fact that divine assistance
does not dispense with human effort.

The Holy Spirit assists the teaching authority of the Church *in and
through the human*, not apart from it or in spite of it. As Catholics we
assume that the Spirit is present and active in official Church teachers as
they carry out their role. But we also believe the same Spirit is present and
active in the hearts of *all* the faithful.

Therefore, just as members of the Church cannot readily assume that
they are right and Church teaching wrong, so official teachers cannot rule
out the possibility that they may be wrong and ordinary believers right
when there is real difficulty with a particular teaching. So, while rightly
relying on the assistance of the Holy Spirit, the pope and bishops must do
their very human homework. They must seek the facts thoroughly; they
must rigorously examine and assess all data. Only then can they formulate
and communicate official teaching.

LISTENING TO CHRIST — TOGETHER

In the light of the Good News, the Church seeks to proclaim gospel
values — how we can live as Jesus lived, in faithful response to the
Father's call and open to the Spirit's guidance. This teaching mission has
three phases, and each of us has a role in the process.

1) The Role of the Official Teachers. The pope and bishops are
responsible for teaching gospel values to people of every country and culture. They draw on many sources: Scripture above all, the Church's living
tradition, theologians. They need to be intimately in touch with the experience of the faithful, the thinking of philosophers, and all the developments
of technology.

To ignore any of these sources would jeopardize the effectiveness of
Church teaching. The Church exists in the world, not in a vacuum; its teaching is *historically conditioned*. It cannot ignore the rootedness in space and

time that has, over the centuries, altered its understanding of such issues as slavery, war, interest on loans, and the role of women in society.

Adapting moral teaching to historical conditions does not mean watering down the Gospel. The Gospel is never easy to live. It always involves conversion, discipleship, the cross. It demands giving our life for others, seeking the Kingdom first, becoming poor, humble, simple, merciful. So the Church's teaching must ever be *challenging and prophetic*, calling us to change our minds and hearts and life-styles and struggle to grow.

Finally, the Church's teaching is necessarily *general and abstract* because it is addressed to the whole world — people of all countries and cultures, children and adults at different stages of faith development. Church teaching concentrates on what ought to be and how people ought to live, *all things being equal*.

2) The Role of Theologians and Preachers. In flesh-and-blood reality, all things often are not equal. Thus the translation of Church teaching into the lived reality of people's lives is an important and necessary step which the teaching itself cannot accomplish. This is the task of theologians and preachers.

Theologians are concerned with the meaning of a particular teaching, its relationship to the Gospel, to other Church teachings, to Tradition, and to other human sciences. They examine a teaching's implications for daily life and its place on a scale of gospel values. Their loyalty to the Church demands that they all use their talents to critique the teachings of the Church they love and cherish. The effectiveness and fruitfulness of Church teaching is at stake.

From preaching at Mass to conducting retreats, from large group lectures to small adult education classes, *preachers* play a vital role in translating official teaching and helping people apply it to the circumstances of their lives.

A bishop depends on those who preach and teach in his diocese to fulfill his official teaching function. Preachers must make every effort to understand official teaching and to communicate it realistically and effectively. They need to be in touch with the people to whom they preach and be aware how their own personal opinions and prejudices affect the way they preach and what they preach. These preachers have the power to inform, to challenge and to encourage growth — or to distort and deaden the Good News.

3) The Role of Personal Conscience. Official teaching is useless if it fails to influence people's lives. The best theology, the most effective preaching is empty if it does not help people live and choose in the light of gospel values. The third and most important phase of the Church's teaching mission is the individual believer's response to Church teaching.

We may be turned off by the classical method or its language; we may reject this way of stating moral teaching. Yet, if we refuse to hear *what* the Church is saying just because we are upset by method or style, we risk missing the vital teaching help of the Church and suffering serious consequences in trying to respond to Christ's call.

Each of us must seek to be "teachable" — open, willing, even eager to hear the teaching of the Church, even when it requires reexamining our values, opinions and conduct. Our duty in conscience is to *know* the official teaching of the Church. This means getting to the heart of the matter to discern the values being taught.

With this kind of attitude, we are "loyal" to the Church even when we are unable to agree with some aspect or method of Church teaching. Such an attitude keeps us sincerely concerned, respectful and involved — ready to achieve a wedding of Church teaching and personal conscience which will become evident in our behavior.

To achieve that wedding — to assimilate Church teaching and translate it into action — is a big order. There is no automatic leap from *knowing* the Church's stance on moral matters to *living* it out. Indeed, there are two major steps we must take before this begins to happen.

First, we *personally* assimilate the Church's values so that they become *our* values. Values don't become ours until we go beyond just "knowing."

What this "beyond knowing" is remains mostly a mystery to us. Somehow it involves openness, sharing, trust, and love between persons. It includes what we mean when we say that "actions speak louder than words" or refer to the power of personal example. Somehow it involves the whole question of religious education and formation of conscience. Somehow it involves finding people who embody values in an inspiring, personal way.

Secondly, as values become ours, we discover something of our potential and hear the call to grow; we are moved to seek concrete ways of embodying those values in our lives.

Most of the time we have no difficulty moving through these two steps. Most of the values the Church teaches are neither new to us no foreign to our lives. Church teaching usually just challenges us to keep struggling, to do better.

But once in a while the Church's teaching calls for radical change. Vatican II, for instance, called for changes in our attitudes toward other faiths, more active participation in the Eucharist, a sense of the positive call to holiness (keeping the Commandments is not enough!). Sometimes the Church's teaching is so demanding we try to ignore it. This has been the case, for instance, with the powerful and emphatic papal appeals for social justice in our century.

And sometimes Church teaching brings us to a crisis point, as did *Humanae Vitae*. Its teaching on contraception prompted vast numbers of Catholics to dissent and created serious difficulties for many others who, while assenting, found themselves in such serious conflict situations that they chose to go against this teaching in order to be more faithful to other teachings.

READING   CATHOLIC BISHOPS OF THE UNITED STATES

"How do I know if I've chosen correctly? Is this the morally right thing to do? How do I know if I've chosen the right vocation? How do I know if this course of action, this relationship or this chosen life-style is best for me?" There are few easy answers. Whether one is facing specific moral decisions or broader vocational questions, the Catholic tradition speaks of *discernment* as that process by which a person uses one's own reasoning ability, the sources of divine revelation (Scripture and Tradition), the Church's teaching and guidance, the wise counsel of others, and one's own individual and communal experiences of grace in a sincere effort to choose wisely and well.

Moral decision making is a particular type of discernment process. In order to decide the right course of action, particularly about matters that may be complex or controversial, Catholics must be open to the wisdom of God manifest in all these sources — one's family, the Church, the Word of God, the sacraments, communal and private prayer, the stories of the saints. At the same time, data from the physical sciences, information from the social sciences, and the insights of human reason can all contribute to one's discovering moral truth.

The bishops gathered at the Second Vatican Council reaffirmed that Christian morality is determined by *objective standards*. "These, based on the nature of the human person and his or her acts," (*Pastoral Constitution in the Modern World*, n. 51) are not intended to preempt human evaluation and discernment, but neither are they reducible solely to sincere intentions or an evaluation of motives.

The Catholic tradition has generally accepted a tiered or sequential approach to Christian ethics, as reflected in the traditional levels of natural law theory. Certain values and derived norms remain timeless and absolute.

At the most basic or objective level are certain principles and values that reflect human nature as imprinted by the design and will of the Creator. The belief that "good is to be sought and evil avoided" is one such fundamental principle.

Similarly, the inherent and abiding worth of such basic values as life, love, and truth are indisputable. Each is a constitutive dimension of human well-being to be preserved and fostered if one is to be a responsible and virtuous person. People of all races, nations, and times have been able to discover and affirm these as true. The Church holds that "there can be no real conflict between the teaching of reason and faith correctly understood" (*Faithful to Each Other Forever, n.* 27). Whether through reasoned reflection or Spirit-inspired revelation, *or both*, humanity can discover, at least in general outline, the meaning of life, the image of God incarnate in the human heart and history.

In some instances, the linkage between a core value and the subsequent positive or negative norm derived from it is so self-evident that the prescription or proscription shares the absoluteness of the value itself. For example, if one accepts that human life is a value, that a certain dignity adheres innately to all living members of the human species, then certain actions, particularly if specified carefully, would in all cases be right or wrong. Thus, the Church holds that the direct killing of the innocent (e.g., abortion, euthanasia, murder, bombing aimed at noncombatants) as well as all directly intended bodily harm to innocent persons (e.g., rape, child or spouse abuse, and torture) are always and everywhere morally wrong.

In other instances, the linkage between fundamental values, norms for behavior, and specific case applications, while real, is more difficult to discern. While we agree that one should always do the "loving thing" or the "life-respecting thing," determining what that means in terms of a given case or context may not be so self-evident. For example, when, if ever, it is "loving" or "life-respecting" to cease life-sustaining treatment on a terminally ill patient? While the Church believes there are still objectively right and wrong answers to such moral dilemmas, the process of moving from absolute values to general norms to specific case judgments requires the virtue of *prudence*. Prudence refers to the ability to exercise judgment in practical matters. Prudence is one of the four cardinal or hinge virtues of the Christian tradition.

John Paul II notes that this prudential or providential discernment process is accomplished through the "sense of faith," which is a gift given by the Holy Spirit to all the faithful. "The Church, therefore, does not accomplish this discernment only through the pastors, who teach in the name and with the power of Christ, but also through the laity" (*Familiaris Consortio*, n. 5).

Still, as the bishops reaffirmed at Vatican II, there is a special teaching role or office within the Church, entrusted to the bishops in communion with the pope. "Endowed with the authority of Christ," it is our responsibility, "by the light of the Holy Spirit," to discern and to teach the faith that is to be believed and put into practice (*Dogmatic Constitution on the Church*, n. 25). It is our unique duty, in conjunction with the Holy Father and other bishops of the world, "to ensure that the Church remains in the truth of Christ" and to lead the People of God ever more deeply into that truth through "an even more mature evangelical discernment" (*Familiaris Consortio*, n. 5).

Finally, there is the area of subjective responsibility. The Church has consistently taught that a person of sincere conscience may have perceived and acted on a moral situation in a manner inconsistent with the teaching of the Church. Still, provided she or he did so with no intentional malice or desire to do wrong, the Christian tradition has recognized mitigated *subjective* culpability for a decision that *objectively* is wrong and ought not to have been made. Subjective culpability is determined by how diligently one strives to form correctly his or her conscience and how sincerely one follows that conscience.

Whether choosing a vocation or making a moral decision that relates to or affects one's vocation, each person must live with and stand by his own discernment or perception of God's will. In either case, "the art of discernment of spirits comes into play. If the content of the experience is in harmony with the gospel data of revelation and tradition and results in a rekindling of faith, strengthening of hope, and fostering of love, than it probably is an experience of God. A sense of greater integrity, peace, and joy or a renewed call to a personal conversion of heart are validating qualities" (*Spiritual Renewal of the American Priesthood*, n. 44).

Ultimately, each person must discern his or her own moral decisions and wider vocational calling. With all the input and support possible, both from individuals and communities, one must still face the future based on decisions made before God in the recesses of one's own heart. As the bishops at Vatican II phrased it, "Conscience is the most secret core and sanctuary of a person. There one is alone with God, whose voice echoes in the depths" (*To Live is Christ*, n. 14).

> *Moral Decision Making and Personal Discernment:*
> *A Catholic Approach (Excerpts).*

HOW I GROW

1. The most important insights I learned about moral decision-making...

_____
_____
_____
_____
_____
_____
_____
_____
_____
_____
_____

2. Ways I can use these insights in my life and in my ministry...

_____
_____
_____
_____
_____
_____
_____
_____
_____

3. Questions I need to explore in future learning:

_____
_____
_____
_____
_____
_____
_____
_____
_____
_____

8

CATHOLIC
SOCIAL TEACHING

WHERE I STAND

1. Jesus addressed social issues when he...

2. It is important for the Church to speak out and address social issues because...

3. I seek to work for justice and peace, serve those in need, and defend the life, dignity, and rights of people by...

4. The most important themes of the Church's social teachings are...

5. Understanding Catholic social teachings is difficult because...

6. Catholic social teaching challenges me to...

READING   CATHOLIC BISHOPS OF THE UNITED STATES

Our faith calls us to work for justice; to serve those in need; to pursue peace; and to defend the life, dignity, and rights of all our sisters and brothers. This is the call of Jesus, the challenge of the prophets, and the living tradition of our Church.

Across this country and around the world, the Church's social ministry is a story of growing vitality and strength, of remarkable compassion, courage, and creativity. It is the everyday reality of providing homeless and hungry people with decent shelter and needed help, of giving pregnant

women and their unborn children lifegiving alternatives, of offering
refugees welcome, and so much more. It is believers advocating in the public arena for human life wherever it is threatened, for the rights of workers
and for economic justice, for peace and freedom around the world, and for
"liberty and justice for all" here at home. It is empowering and helping
poor and vulnerable people to realize their dignity in inner cities, in rural
communities, and in lands far away. It is the everyday commitment of
countless people, parishes and programs, local networks and national structures — a tradition of caring service, effective advocacy, and creative
action.

At the heart of this commitment is a set of principles, a body of
thought, and a call to action known as Catholic social teaching. 1991
marked the 100th anniversary of the first great modern social encyclical,
Rerum Novarum, and the Church celebrated a century of powerful social
teaching.

SOCIAL MISSION AND SOCIAL TEACHING

The story of the Church's social mission is both old and new, both a
tradition to be shared and a challenge to be fulfilled. The Church's social
ministry is:

* *founded on the life and words of Jesus Christ*, who came "to bring glad
tidings of the poor... liberty to captives...recovery of sight to the blind..."
(Lk 4:18-19), and who identified himself in the powerful parable of the
Last Judgement with the hungry, the homeless, the stranger, "the least of
these" (cf. Mt 25:45);

* *inspired by the passion for justice of the Hebrew prophets* and the scrip-
tural call to care for the weak and to "let justice surge like water" (Am
5:24);

* *shaped by the social teaching of our Church*, papal encyclicals, conciliar
documents, and episcopal statements that, especially over the last century,
have explored, expressed, and affirmed the social demands of our faith,
insisting that work for justice and peace and care for the poor and vulnerable are the responsibility of every Christian; and

* *lived by the People of God*, who seek to build up the Kingdom of God, to
live our faith in the world and to apply the values of the Scriptures and the
teaching of the Church in our own families and parishes, in our work and
service and in local communities, the nation, and the world.

The social dimensions of our faith have taken on special urgency and
clarity over this last century. Guided by Pope Leo XIII and his successors,

by the Second Vatican Council, and by the bishops of the Church, Catholics
have been challenged to understand more clearly and act more concretely
on the social demands of the Gospel. This tradition calls all members of the
Church, rich and poor alike, to work to eliminate the occurrence and effects
of poverty, to speak out against injustice, and to shape a more caring society and a more peaceful world.

Together we seek to meet this challenge. Much, however, remains to
be done if social doctrine is to become a truly vital and integral part of
Catholic life and if we are to meet its challenges in our own lives and social
structures. For too many, Catholic social teaching is still an unknown
resource. It is sometimes misunderstood as a peripheral aspect rather than
as an integral and constitutive element of our faith. The challenge of the
1971 Synod to make working for justice a constitutive dimension of
responding to the Gospel should be emphasized in our society, where many
see religion as something personal and private. This is tragic since the
Catholic social vision offers words of hope, a set of principles and direc-
tions for action to a world longing for greater freedom, justice, and peace.

Catholic social teaching is a powerful and liberating message in a
world of stark contradictions: a world of inspiring new freedom and linger-
ing oppression, of peaceful change and violent conflict, of remarkable economic progress for some and tragic misery and poverty for many others.
Our teaching is a call to conscience, compassion, and creative action in a
world confronting the terrible tragedy of widespread abortion, the haunting
reality of hunger and homelessness, and the evil of continuing prejudice
and poverty. Our teaching lifts up the moral and human dimensions of
major public issues, examining "the signs of the times" through the values
of the Scriptures, the teaching of the Church, and the experience of the
People of God.

BASIC THEMES

Our Catholic social teaching is more than a set of documents. It is a
living tradition of thought and action. The Church's social vision has developed and grown over time, responding to changing circumstances and
emerging problems — including developments in human work, new economic questions, war and peace in a nuclear age, and poverty and development in a shrinking world. While the subjects have changed, some basic
principles and themes have emerged within this tradition.

A. THE LIFE AND DIGNITY OF THE HUMAN PERSON

In the Catholic social vision, the human person is central, the clearest reflection of God among us. Each person possesses a basic dignity that comes from God, not from any human quality or accomplishment, not from race or gender, age or economic status. The test of every institution or policy is whether it enhances or threatens human life and human dignity. We believe people are more important than things.

B. THE RIGHTS AND RESPONSIBILITIES OF THE HUMAN PERSON

Flowing from our God-given dignity, each person has basic rights and responsibilities. These include the rights to freedom of conscience and religious liberty, to raise a family, to immigrate, to live free from unfair discrimination, and to have a share of earthly good sufficient for oneself and one's family. People have a fundamental right to life and to those things that make life truly human: food, clothing, housing, health care, education, security, social services, and employment. Corresponding to these rights are duties and responsibilities — to one another, to our families, and to the larger society, to respect the rights of others and to work the common good.

C. THE CALL TO FAMILY, COMMUNITY, AND PARTICIPATION

The human person is not only sacred, but social. We realize our dignity and rights in relationship with others in community. No community is more central than the family; it needs to be supported, not undermined. It is the basic cell of society, and the state has an obligation to support the family. The family has major contributions to make in addressing questions of social justice. It is where we learn and act on our values. What happens in the family is at the basis of a truly human social life. We also have the right and responsibility to participate in and contribute to the broader communities in society. The state and other institutions of political and economic life, with both their limitations and obligations, are instruments to protect the life, dignity, and rights of the person; promote the well-being of our families and communities; and pursue the common good. Catholic social teaching does offer clear guidance on the role of government. When basic human needs are not being met by private initiative, then people must work through their government, at appropriate levels, to meet those needs. A central test of political, legal, and economic institutions is what they do *to* people, what they do *for* people, and how people *participate* in them.

D. THE DIGNITY OF WORK AND THE RIGHTS OF WORKERS

Work is more than a way to make a living; it is an expression of our dignity and a form of continuing participation in God's creation. People have the right to decent and productive work, to decent and fair wages, to private property and economic initiative. Workers have the strong support of the Church in forming and joining union and worker associations of their choosing in the exercise of their dignity and rights. These values are at the heart of *Rerum Novarum* and other encyclicals on economic justice. In Catholic teaching, the economy exists to serve people, not the other way around.

E. THE OPTION FOR THE POOR AND VULNERABLE

Poor and vulnerable people have a special place in Catholic social teaching. A basic moral test of a society is how its most vulnerable members are faring. This is not a new insight; it is the lesson of the parable of the Last Judgment (see Mt 25). Our tradition calls us to put the needs of the poor and vulnerable first. As Christians, we are called to respond to the needs of all our sisters and brothers, but those with the greatest needs require the greatest response. We must seek creative ways to expand the emphasis of our nation's founders on individual rights and freedom by extending democratic ideals to economic life and thus ensure that the basic requirements for life with dignity are accessible to all.

F. SOLIDARITY

We are one human family, whatever our national, racial, ethnic, economic, and ideological differences. We are our brothers' and sisters' keepers (cf. Gn 4:9). In a linked and limited world, our responsibilities to one another cross national and other boundaries. Violent conflict and the denial of dignity and rights to people anywhere on the globe diminish each of us. This emerging theme of solidarity, so strongly articulated by Pope John Paul II, expresses the core of the Church's concern for world peace, global development, environment, and international human rights. It is the contemporary expression of the traditional Catholic image of the *Mystical Body*. "Loving our neighbor" has global dimensions in an interdependent world.

There are other significant values and principles that also shape and guide the Church's traditional social teaching, but these six themes are central parts of the tradition. We encourage you to read, reflect on, and discuss the documents that make up this tradition (see * p. 71). They are a rich resource touching a wide variety of vital, complex, and sometimes controversial concerns. This teaching offers not an alternative social system, but fundamental values that test every system, every nation, and every community. It puts the needs of the poor first. It values persons over things. It emphasizes morality over technology, asking not simply what *can* we do, but what *ought* we do. It calls us to measure our lives not by what we have, but by who we are; how we love one another; and how we contribute to the common good, to justice in our community, and to peace in our world.

THE CONTINUING CHALLENGE

This long tradition has led our Church over the last century to support workers and unions actively in the exercise of their rights; to work against racism and bigotry of every kind; to condemn abortion, the arms race, and other threats to human life; and to pursue a more just society and a more peaceful world. These principles are the foundation of the Catholic community's many efforts to serve the poor, immigrants, and other vulnerable people. We know our individual and institutional acts of charity are requirements of the Gospel. They are essential but not sufficient. Our efforts to feed the hungry, shelter the homeless, welcome the stranger, and serve the poor and vulnerable must be accompanied by concrete efforts to address the causes of human suffering and injustice. We believe advocacy and action to carry out our principles and constructive dialogue about how best to do this both strengthen our Church and enrich our society. We are called to transform our hearts and our social structures, to renew the face of the earth.

Social justice is not something Catholics pursue simply through parish committees and diocesan programs although these structures can help us to act on our faith. Our social vocation takes flesh in our homes and schools, businesses and unions, offices and factories, colleges and universities, and in community organizations and professional groups. As believers, we are called to bring our values into the marketplace and the political arena, into community and family life, using our everyday opportunities and responsibilities, our voices and votes to defend human life, human dignity, and human rights. We are called to be a leaven, applying Christian values and virtues in every aspect of our lives.

We are also called to weave our social teaching into every dimension of Catholic life, especially worship, education, planning, and evangelization. The Holy Father can teach; bishops can preach; but unless our social doctrine comes alive in personal conversion and common action, it will lack credibility and effectiveness. We need to build on the experience and commitment of so many parishes where worship consistently reflects the gospel call to continuing conversion, caring service, and creative action. The call to penance and reconciliation must include both the social and the individual dimensions of sin. Our schools and catechetical efforts should regularly share our social teaching. We know that liturgy, religious education, and other apostolates that ignore the social dimensions of our faith are neither faithful to our traditions nor fully Catholic. We also know that parish life that does not reflect the gospel call to charity and justice neglects an essential dimension of pastoral ministry. We cannot celebrate a faith we do not practice. We cannot proclaim a gospel we do not live. We must work together to ensure that we continue to move together from strong words about charity and justice to effective action, from official statements to creative ministry at every level of the Church's life.

CONCLUSION

As we celebrate this century of social teaching, it is important to remember who calls us to this task and why we pursue it. Our work for social justice is first and foremost a work of faith, a profoundly religious task. It is Jesus who calls us to this mission, not any political or ideological agenda. We are called to bring the healing hand of Christ to those in need; the courageous voice of the prophet to those in power; and the gospel message of love, justice, and peace to an often suffering world.

This is not a new challenge. It is the enduring legacy of Pope Leo XIII, who a century ago defended the rights of workers. It is the lasting message of Pope John XXIII, who called for real peace based on genuine respect for human rights. It is the continuing challenge of Pope Paul VI, who declared, "if you want peace, work for justice." It is the commitment of the Second Vatican Council, which declared, "the joys and hopes, the griefs and anxieties" of people of this age, especially those who are poor or afflicted, are "the joys and hopes, the griefs and anxieties of the followers of Christ." It is the powerful vision of our present Holy Father, Pope John Paul II, who by work and deed calls for a new global solidarity that respects and enhances the dignity of every human person.

Most of all, it is the challenge of our Lord Jesus Christ, who laid out our continuing challenge in the Sermon on the Mount. Let us explore together what it means to be "poor in spirit" in a consumer society; to "comfort those who suffer" in our midst; to "show mercy" in an often unforgiving world; to "hunger and thirst for justice" in a nation still challenged by hunger and homelessness, poverty and prejudice; to be "peacemakers" in an often violent and fearful world; and to be the "salt of the earth and the light of the world" in our own time and place.

We hope and pray that we will become a family of faith evermore committed to the defense of the life, the dignity, and the rights of every human person and a community of genuine solidarity, working every day to build a world of greater justice and peace for all God's children.

* Among the major topics addressed by these documents are a wide range of economic concerns: the roles of workers and owners, the rights to private property and its limitations, employment and unemployment, economic rights and initiative, debt and development, poverty and wealth, urban and rural concerns. Central concerns include major questions touching human life: abortion, euthanasia, health care, the death penalty, and the violence of war and crime. Also emphasized are issues of discrimination and diversity: racism, ethnic prejudice, cultural pluralism, the dignity and equality of women, and the rights of immigrants and refugees.

Social teaching also addresses broader questions of religious liberty, political freedom, the common good, the role of the state, subsidiarity and socialization, church-state relations, and political responsibility. A major focus has been the pursuit of peace, disarmament, and the use of force and nonviolence, as well as international justice. An emerging issue is the environment.

A Century of Social Teaching
(A Pastoral Message of the Catholic Bishops)

HOW I GROW

1. The most important insights I learned about Catholic social teaching...

_____
_____
_____
_____
_____
_____

2. Ways I can use these insights in my life and in my ministry...

_____
_____
_____
_____
_____

3. Questions I need to explore in future learning:

_____
_____
_____
_____
_____

9
CATHOLIC IDENTITY

WHERE I STAND

1. When I was a child, being Catholic meant...

2. Being a Catholic today is important for me because...

3. Several ways I express or live my Catholic faith....

4. Several good reasons for being Catholic today are...

5. Being Catholic today is difficult because...

ESSAY   RICHARD ROHR, OFM, AND JOSEPH MARTOS

Many of us who are older and who grew up in the Church before the Second Vatican Council never seriously faced the question, "Why be Catholic?" Not being Catholic was almost unthinkable for us, as unthinkable as not being American.

Yet today, many people are in fact asking the question, "Why be Catholic?" They ask that question when their parish liturgy becomes intolerably boring, when they disagree with the pope or bishops on social issues, when they divorce and remarry and are told that they can't receive Communion. Often the question is, "Why *remain* Catholic?"

Following Vatican II, Catholics rightly rethought the narrow approach they had taken with the belief that outside the Church there is no salvation. They broadened the idea of salvation so that it could embrace God's love for all Christians, and indeed all persons of good faith.

If good people of other religious persuasions can be saved, then why be — or remain — Catholic?

The answer is Catholicism's rich 2,000-year tradition of living the Gospel. And this tradition is a "wisdom tradition." Unlike some of the younger Churches which sprang up after the Protestant Reformation and often splintered into further divisions, Catholicism has maintained unity *and* diversity over the course of 20 centuries. It embraces the wisdom of the ancient world, the Middle Ages and modern times.

We can summarize the wisdom of the Catholic tradition under eight headings. Each of these values represents not only a challenge but also a good reason for being Catholic.

1. AN OPTIMISTIC VIEW OF CREATION

There is an old poem that reads: "Wherever the Catholic sun does shine, There's music, laughter and good red wine. At least, I've always found it so: Benedicamus Domino!"

The last line is Latin for "Let us bless the Lord!" And this poem captures a very basic Catholic sensibility: that creation is *good*. It represents God's wisdom as God looked out on the world just after its creation and pronounced it "very good" (Gn 1:31).

From time to time some Christians have not believed in the full goodness of creation. Early Gnostics and other "super-spiritual" groups felt that the material world was bad — but they were regarded as heretics by the majority of the Christians. In the Middle Ages some monks thought that sex was sinful — but the Church replied by affirming the sacramentality of marriage. A few centuries ago Catholic puritans (called Jansenists) condemned all worldliness and sensuality — but the Church officially rejected their teaching.

Many of us who come from northern European backgrounds (especially Irish and German) inherited this Jansenistic negativity anyway. Priests, nuns, and others who shaped attitudes often portrayed sexual misconduct as the worst possible sin. As Americans we also adopted a good deal of puritanism from our Protestant neighbors. Our immigrant grandparents didn't want to appear less moral than the people around them!

The older and larger Catholic tradition, however, has Mediterranean roots. Palestinians and Greeks, Italians and French, Spanish and Portuguese have generally been more comfortable with their bodies than northern Europeans. Peasants and poor people — most "Catholic countries" even today are poor — have always been among those who best appreciate the good things that nature has to offer. Food and drink, sex and children are the simple but most basic pleasures that life can give us. They are, after all, gifts from God intended for our enjoyment when wisely used.

This is why Catholicism is fundamentally sacramental. A sacrament is a sign of God's goodness to us. Catholic wisdom says that the world and everything in it is a gift from God and a sign of God. The seven sacraments we celebrate in church use water and oil, bread and wine, and human touch as signs of God's graciousness. Catholics see God shining through all of creation, and so they use the gifts of creation in their most important rituals. Thus Catholics are very comfortable bringing sculpture, painting, stained-glass windows, music, drama and other elements of the created world into their worship.

2. A UNIVERSAL VISION

The original meaning of the word *catholic* is "universal." The Church was first called catholic in ancient times after the entire Roman Empire had been converted to Christianity. The first universal Church council met in Nicaea in the year 325, and in similar councils the world's bishops formulated the Church's catholic faith. The summary of that worldwide faith is Nicene Creed which we say at Mass every Sunday.

The Catholic Church still has a worldwide faith, and the Church's vision is still universal. Pope John Paul II travels every year to meet Catholics around the world. The Pope's vision and the Church's vision stretch beyond national boundaries. Wherever the Pope goes he is greeted by Catholics — our brothers and sisters in the Lord.

The Catholic Church is not a national Church. It is one of the few truly international institutions in the world today. The Catholic Church is also a multicultural Church. It is not just European and American but also Latino and African and Asian. People of every race and culture embrace the Catholic faith and are embraced by the universal Church.

Because the Church is universal, it calls us to a universal vision. As the world gets smaller every year, we need to regard everyone in it as our neighbor. Our faith is already larger than most of us realize, challenging our narrowness and preparing us for global citizenship. The pastoral letters of the U.S. bishops on peacemaking and on economic justice seek to promote this global outlook.

If we are truly Catholic, we must look at the world and all people in it from God's perspective, and not from a nationalistic or ethnocentric point of view. The Catholic vision, when fully lived, reflects God's concern for the entire human family.

3. A HOLISTIC OUTLOOK

The Church has always been concerned with holiness. At times in the past people have equated holiness with becoming a plaster saint, aloof from others and abstracted from life. Today we realize that holiness is wholeness. If we look at the Catholic past, we see that this wholeness has always been the ideal.

Catholicism has never said you need to be a secluded monk or a cloistered nun to be holy. When we look at the Church's calendar of saints, we see fishermen and farmers, husbands and wives, rich and poor, soldiers and scholars, even kings and queens honored there. Everyone is called to achieve his/her fullest potential, to be a truly whole and holy person.

This holistic spirituality is very rewarding, but it is also very demanding. Catholic holiness is not a Jesus-and-me attitude. It's not enough to go to Church on Sunday and leave the rest of your life unchanged. True holiness requires a conversion of the whole person, a transformation of the total personality, a concern for bodily as well as spiritual health, and a balance between prayer and action. This may require a conversion of our life-style no matter where we live or what we do for a living.

4. PERSONAL GROWTH

The Catholic vision of human potential begins with conversion — a conversion that is ongoing. It sees life as a process of continuous conversion and growth. There is no one moment when a Catholic claims to be "saved," as fundamentalists do. The stories of the saints show that they continuously strove for holiness. Even the Catholic devotion known as the Stations of the Cross suggests that the Christian life is a process, a journey that goes through stages, introducing us to different challenges, pitfalls and personalities along the way. Those who persevere in fidelity and trust enter more deeply into God's life.

Fortunately, our salvation and our happiness do not depend on us alone. God is with us and lovingly takes the initiative in offering us salvation and calling us to holiness. This is the meaning of grace. Grace is God's invitation and power reaching into us. We have to open ourselves to God in order to be filled with the Spirit. We have to cooperate with grace.

Curiously, our cooperation is not so much a "doing" as a "not doing." The wisdom of the saints is that they stopped long enough to listen to God in their hearts and let God tell them how to be truly happy. Growth in the Spirit, growth in spiritual perfection (as we used to call it), is the same as growing in Christ. It means surrendering our own shortsightedness about what we can be and entering into the process of becoming like Christ.

Paradoxically, personal fulfillment means abandoning ourselves and putting others first. In the Catholic tradition, ultimate satisfaction is promised to those who give up their desire for self-satisfaction. This is part of the meaning of crucifixion. The cross leads to resurrection, to new life. When we let go of ourselves, our lives become filled with grace. The lives of St. Francis of Assisi, Pope John XXIII, and Mother Teresa of Calcutta radiate a grace that people of all religious traditions admire.

5. SOCIAL TRANSFORMATION

Society has been transformed again and again by Christianity. Jesus proclaimed the coming of God's Kingdom, and the Church has tried again and again to make the Kingdom real. The Church has always been concerned for human betterment.

In ancient Rome the Church protested against gladiator fights and other forms of killing for sport. In the Middle Ages, prophetic voices in the Church were raised to defend the peasants against the tyranny of the nobles. Monasteries were the first hospitals for the sick and the first hotels for weary pilgrims. The Church has always cared for widows and orphans. It has fought against slavery, against the dehumanization of factory workers and against the exploitation of migrant laborers. In the 1960's Catholics marched for civil rights, and today they march for the right to life in its many forms as well as for many other social causes.

This concern for the poor and the underprivileged springs directly from the Catholic understanding of holistic growth and universal salvation. God wants everyone to reach full potential as a human being created in God's image. This means first having basic human needs met and then growing to full maturity in Christ through meeting the needs of others. The Gospel is a message to be shared at every level of human life, and the Good News is that God's power is available to redeem the world.

Accepting the Catholic vision means never accepting things the way they are. People are always hurting and suffering oppression. People are always needing to be healed and set free. To stop much of the pain and hurt, society itself has to be transformed. Being Catholic means standing with those social reformers who have always wanted to change the world, making it more like God's Kingdom.

6. A COMMUNAL SPIRIT

To a great extent, we in America have lost the Catholic sense of community. Our large parishes are often very impersonal; at Sunday Mass most people feel more like an anonymous audience than a faith community.

The reason for this is that we Catholics have bought into the American myths of rugged individualism and middle-class success. We believe that we have to make it on our own and that, if we are successful, we should have our own separate houses, our own private cars, and all the appliances to live comfortably by ourselves.

This individualism and self-centeredness is disastrous for community. It is not the ideal taught us by our Catholic tradition. The Christian way of living is communitarian. Early Christians were so connected to one another that St. Paul called each community a "body of Christ." When the Church grew larger, some Spirit-led Christians left the cities to live together in the countryside. They worked and prayed together in what were then called monasteries. Today we might call them Christian communes.

Monasteries were centers of Christian living all around Europe in the Middle Ages. In time, community-minded Christians discovered other ways of joining their lives together even in cities. Usually these communities focused on some apostolic work such as caring for the sick, the homeless or the uneducated. That's the origin of today's religious orders.

The peculiarly Catholic gift to the Church is community. Protestantism broke away from the tradition of monasteries and religious orders. This is not to say religious orders are the only way of achieving a communal spirit within the Catholic and Protestant traditions. Indeed, in many cases, Catholics can learn much from the degree of "fellowship" achieved in numerous Protestant communions. However, Catholic theology — if not always our practice — challenges us to see the Church as community.

Today, when many of our traditional orders have grown to institutional proportions, Catholics are searching for new forms of communal life. Many in religious orders are moving into smaller, more personal living arrangements. Prayer groups, spiritual movements, and base communities are all attempts to revive this Catholic charism in a modern setting. In our individualistic society, there is a felt need for this gift of community.

7. A PROFOUND SENSE OF HISTORY

The Catholic Church has been around for a long time — nearly 20 centuries. That's four or five times the age of the oldest Protestant denominations, and 10 times as old as the United States. Belonging to a Church with that sort of history gives us a unique historical perspective. At least, it should!

Too often we as Americans live in the immediacy of the present. We forget that most of the problems we face today as individuals and as a society have been addressed by the Church for centuries and centuries. How quickly we forget that the English once were our enemies, as were the Germans and the Japanese even more recently. How quickly we forget the conversion of Russia some 1,000 years ago and that the majority of people who live in Russia are Christians. When we forget that most people who would be killed by our nuclear attack are our sisters and brothers in Christ, it is easy to picture them as our enemies. Yet our history shows that those who were once considered enemies can become friends.

In its 2,000 years, the Church has lived under kings and emperors, in democracies and dictatorships, under capitalism and communism. The Catholic perspective on history shows that we do not have to fear any political or economic system. The Gospel can be lived in any place, at any time, under any conditions. Our strong sense of roots and continuity with a rich Catholic past is certainly a value to be cherished.

8. A RESPECT FOR HUMAN KNOWLEDGE

After philosophy (which dates back to pre-Christian times) the oldest intellectual discipline in the world is theology. Catholicism has never been a matter of blind faith. One of the earliest definitions of theology is "faith seeking understanding." The Catholic ideal is to respect reason and promote understanding.

When barbarian tribes swept across Europe and caused the fall of the Roman Empire, monks carefully copied fragile manuscripts so that ancient science would not be lost. Even in the "Dark Ages" that bred the anti-intellectualism of the Inquisition, Christian scholars were founding schools which eventually became the great universities of Europe. Despite the obtuseness of the Church officials who condemned Galileo, modern science grew out of the efforts of Christians to understand the universe that God created.

St. Augustine tried to understand all of history from the perspective of Catholic faith. St. Thomas Aquinas studied all medieval science before writing his great *Summa Theologica*, a four-volume "summary" of theology. Our Catholic scholars advanced medicine, law, astronomy, and biology. Catholics believe that if they are firmly grounded in their faith, they do not have to feel threatened by any scientific knowledge. Teilhard de Chardin integrated evolution into his Christian understanding of the cosmos.

This openness to human knowledge is not true of all Christians today. Some fundamentalists close their eyes against the evidence for evolution. Others insist so strongly on the truth of the Bible that they have little respect for what psychology and sociology can teach us. Some Catholics fall into this same trap regarding Church dogmas. But the broader Catholic wisdom is that all truth comes from God, whether it is revealed or discovered.

OUR HERITAGE POINTS TO CHRIST

To be truly Catholic therefore means to enter into the Catholic wisdom tradition. It means appreciating all of creation and looking at the world from a universal perspective. It means adopting a holistic outlook that encourages personal growth and social transformation. It means building community and learning from history. It means not being afraid to ask questions about faith, about the Church, or about the world in which we live.

Yet all this heritage is pointless unless it also points us to Christ, and to living the Gospel. The reason for accepting the Catholic tradition is to learn better from our rich past how to live our faith more deeply today.

HOW I GROW

1. The most important insights I learned about Catholic identity...

_____
_____
_____
_____
_____

2. Ways I can use these insights in my life and in my ministry...

_____
_____
_____
_____
_____

3. Questions I need to explore in future learning:

_____
_____
_____
_____
_____